Before the
Dust Settles

Published in 2023 by Welford Publishing

Copyright © Martin Ridley 2023

ISBN: Paperback 978-1-7390970-5-9

Martin Ridley has asserted his right to be identified as the author of this Work in accordance with the Copyright, Designs and Patents Act 1988.

All rights reserved. No part of this publication may be reproduced, stored in a retrieval system, or transmitted in any form or by any means, electronic, mechanical, photocopying, recording or otherwise, without the prior permission of the copyright owner.

A catalogue for this book is available from the British Library.

Editor Alison Stead

Before the Dust Settles

Martin Ridley

Disclaimer

This book is designed to provide helpful information on the subjects discussed. It is general reference information which should not be used to diagnose any medical problem and is not intended as a substitute for consulting with a medical or professional practitioner.

Some names and identifying details have been changed to protect the privacy of the individuals.

Dedication

I would like to dedicate this book to anyone that is lost, struggling and looking for answers. To anyone that has met with Alzheimer's, lost a baby or suffering with grief from any loss of a loved one.

I also dedicate this book to anyone that's wondering where they belong or how they can fit in. I dedicate this book to anybody who feels like they can't take it anymore and can't go on. Anybody that has or is struggling with any of these things, I dedicate this book to you.

Contents

01.	Despair	9
02.	Finding My Feet Again	22
03.	The Exploration Begins	32
04.	A Night of Testimony	39
05.	Learning Who I Am	45
06.	History That Changed My World	55
07.	Hope of a New Career	69
08.	My Exploration of Faith	78
09.	The Unexpected New Relationship	85
10.	'November Delta Four Six to YF…'	95
11.	That Explains Things	103
12.	A New Life Begins	114
13.	Lessons Learned	139

Acknowledgements 147

About the Author 149

Contact Martin at 151

Chapter 1
Despair

It was early 2017 when I wearily slumped down onto my knees, devoid of hope, and rested my elbows on my bed, while my lifeless eyes looked out of my bedroom window. I joined my hands together, clasping my left hand with my right, almost as if trying to comfort it. My head fell forward under the weight of my broken spirit and my eyes closed with my eye lids squeezing together from the force of my despair.

Moving around behind their curtains of skin, my eyes searched the darkness of my mind for the words that might be appropriate. Words that might just be able to pull me out of the hell I was in, back up on to my feet again. Then the words came to me, and I built up the courage to speak them out into the air, to no-one, to nothing. "Dear God … If you're there, if you really do exist, I could really do with your help right now. I can't take this anymore, I've had enough. Please help me. Amen".

I didn't believe in God, but I was willing to try anything at that point. I would have felt relief to no longer be alive at all. I would've just been glad to escape this life, to not have to deal with it anymore. I often thought about it. Wishing I wasn't here anymore, free from all of the misery, grief and failure - what was so good about being alive anyway? Nothing, as far as I could tell.

I was at the end of my ability to cope, or to see any kind of hope for the future. All I could see was more of the same. I couldn't see any ways forward to improve my situation. I was exhausted and had run out of patience for the life I was stuck in. I couldn't exit stage left though, so that only left one option. That option was to pray in desperation to the God that I didn't believe in. I can't say that I was expecting much from that avenue either.

I was kneeling in the bedroom that I had slept in for about thirty years, in our family home, now just me and my brother living there. I shouldn't even be living there anymore. I was 37, what a complete waste of space, what a joke. I should have left there and moved into my own place many years before that, like everybody else from my year at school had done. Like everyone had probably done from the years below me too. I was such a failure.

I should have had a career as a professional footballer like my dad who played professionally until he was thirty-five, but that ended for me when I was just nineteen. I had the ability to have a career in first team football just not the character, which my dad, in his efforts to help me improve, made clear to me when I was a boy. I wasn't brave enough, confident enough or loud enough. Now here I was at thirty-seven still living at home, knelt in the bedroom that I moved into when I was eight, pathetically asking other peoples' imagination to rescue me from my life, my failures and myself. On my own where nobody else could see or hear me, speaking to the old-fashioned fantasy and disproven creator of the universe. What was I doing?

I got up from my knees, awkwardly pushing up with my hands from my bed to get back to my feet. It was like my head needed a moment to come back to its senses, then I slowly turned and walked over to my bedroom door, pulled it open again and walked back out into my life. I went downstairs, made myself a cup of tea and sat on the sofa in the living room and turned on the TV. My brother came home from football a short while later, none the wiser of where my head was at. As normal he began to take the mick out of me and talk nonsense about nothing in particular. I played along as usual, returning his first serve of banter and then engaging in an ongoing rally. Laughing in the right places and pretending that all was fine.

Monday morning came round again, and it was time to get up and put my shirt and tie on before setting off on the ninety-minute journey to work. It was dark and cold in the mornings, and the bright lights of the other cars overwhelmed my eyes as I drove. I could feel the strain in my head. It should have taken about an hour to work but with the rush hour traffic it always took about ninety minutes. Ninety minutes of continuous concentration as I tried to avoid an accident and stay alive.

I found getting up difficult after another night of not sleeping very well. It was not unusual for me to still be awake into the early hours of the morning, or to wake up hours before I needed to and be unable to get back to sleep. As I tried to get more precious sleep my alarm would go off, I would know that I wasn't ready for it and a feeling of dread for the day soaked through my body. How would I cope and get through it? As I set off to work, I was very aware of my heavy brow and eye lids, and the weight of my arms as they stretched out in front of me to control the steering wheel. I had to make a conscious effort to focus my eyes from their natural state of blurriness - effort that used energy already in short supply.

Months earlier I was in Newcastle-under-Lyme having breakfast in one of the bar/cafes when my phone surprised me with its ring tone, and a phone number on the screen that I didn't recognise.

"Hello?"

"Hi, is that Martin?"

"Yes, it is."

"Hi Martin, it's Gail here regarding your job application."

"Oh hi Gail, are y'alright?"

"Yes I'm good thank you. The reason I'm ringing you is to inform you that you got the job." She said with an excited and happy tone.

"Oh brilliant, thank you." YES!! I was ecstatic and punched the air in celebration.

"Congratulations".

Soon after that call I posted on social media about landing my dream job. I hadn't really had a normal job, so I was thrilled that an employer had taken me on as an employee. More than that though, to be employed by a world-famous organisation in professional golf, and to work in the subject area of coaching within their training department was simply amazing to me! It was my favourite topic and the one that I felt most confident in, so I felt very fortunate to have been employed to work in that area on a daily basis. I thought my work life was sorted and couldn't wait to start.

Months later, I found myself feeling exhausted as I got into my car to drive home from work. The ninety-minute drive home would typically feel longer than the ninety-minute drive to work, especially in the dark. The bright lights were even more draining accompanied by my impatience to get home. When I walked back through our front door, I was already thinking about going to bed. Of course, I needed to get changed and have something to eat before that, but I wasn't sure I had the energy. It felt to me like there was little time between getting home and needing to go to bed. There wasn't enough time to wind down from the day I had just gone through before needing to prepare to do it again.

I was also conscious that I needed to visit my dad. He was now in a home having finally been diagnosed with Alzheimer's, the same illness that had taken our mum from us. I remember when Dad told me on our front lawn that doctors had found a shrinkage to the front of Mum's brain, and that they had diagnosed her with Alzheimer's. It was a warm sunny day in the summer of 2008, but when I heard those words, I suddenly felt cold.

They had known for weeks apparently, if not months, but hadn't told me or my brother because they were trying to protect us from it. That annoyed me a little to be honest, I was 28 years old after all, I was able to handle that information. Parental instinct I guess. It hadn't surprised me when Dad told me, but I was still shocked by the reality of it. Now it was a reality I wondered what it meant. What was going to happen to Mum now? I researched the disease and didn't like what I found out at all. It said that Mum probably had ten years left to live.

Dad couldn't accept her diagnosis, he couldn't even say Alzheimer's - the word was too big and sharp at its edges for him to get it out of his mouth. It was just too upsetting for him, as shown by the tears that pooled in his eyes. He tried to continue life as normal, but he struggled to cope with her as she got worse. At that time, I was working as a professional golf caddie on the Ladies European Tour and later the DP World Tour (as it's called now), so I was away from home quite regularly. When I was at home, I would help with Mum but I could see how much Dad was struggling. It made it hard to go away again but mum insisted that I did. It got to a point though where I felt I had to act. This culminated in me arranging for Mum to be moved into a care home for a week in late February 2012 for respite, roughly four years after her diagnosis.

I found my parents in the local pub and asked Mum to come with me, which she did without protest or query, she trusted me. Dad was the one that protested after coming out to us in the car park, but I eventually convinced him to let us go. It was just for one week, so they could care for her and give him a break. I was determined that this was happening because she needed better care than she was getting. I drove Mum to the care home. I explained who we were at the reception, and they acknowledged that they were expecting us. The lady then showed us to Mum's room.

Mum happily followed the lady to her room and sat on one of the chairs while I sat on the other. She accepted the offer of a cup of tea with a grateful smile and the carer left the room to go and get the drinks sorted. Mum looked at me and smiled. Then she asked me where we were and why we were there. I told her that we were in a care home and that she would be staying there for the week. "Oh", she replied simply, with a slight Yorkshire accent. She smiled at me again with that big smile of hers, which was like a torch for the daytime.

The drinks arrived and the carer spoke with Mum briefly about her staying there for the week, which surprised Mum, then the carer left us so Mum could settle in, and we could talk more by ourselves.

"Where are we and why are we here?" Mum asked me again.

"We're at a care home, it's only a few minutes from our house, they're going to look after you for the week. They will take good care of you here."

"Oh".

She smiled at me, and we sat with our cups of tea and chatted about life for a while.

After about an hour or so I announced to Mum that I was going to have to go now. She then got up and went for her coat too. I explained to her that she would be staying. Her smile dropped to the floor, and she looked at me heartbroken.

"No, not you", she said in a soft voice, like the one person that she thought she could trust had just utterly betrayed her.

"You'll be fine here Mum, it's just for a few days so they can look after you better. I'll be back tomorrow, and we're really close if you need us."

I looked at her hoping to see or hear a response of agreement or forgiveness. I was heartbroken too and felt the lower part of my throat choke up. I tried again to explain what was happening and why, but to little avail. Then I kissed her on the cheek, said goodbye and walked out of the room leaving her there alone. I felt horrible and cruel as I walked to my car with tears in my eyes.

Later that day I showed Dad where Mum was staying and informed him that he could visit her at certain times of the day. Again, I explained that it was just for one week to give him respite and for Mum to get looked after. The next night I was called by the home to come and help them with my dad as he was demanding to take Mum home, which wasn't possible.

When I arrived at the home I found my dad stood outside the front door.

"I want your mum at home Martin, she should be at home with us."

"I know Dad, but it's just for a week so they can look after her and give you a break."

"I didn't ask for a break, I want to take her home."

"I'm sorry Dad but that's not going to be possible, it's just for a few days then she will be back home."

He backed down at this and reluctantly went home, which was a relief for me. I also felt like the bad guy for him too though. I had separated him from his wife without his consent and now he was powerless to do anything about it. As the eldest son, I had adopted the role as the lead for our family because of Dad's poor health. He was also displaying behaviour by this stage which suggested that he might have some form of dementia too. He maintained the legal authority over Mum as her next of kin but wasn't right himself, which made things very difficult for me when I was trying to get Mum more help and support. Unfortunately, we didn't have power of attorney in place because it had been too late when we applied to get it, Mum hadn't been well enough to grant it. That meant everything had to go through my dad.

It was the overspill of my frustration from this situation that led to us being where we were.

Mum's behaviour in the home caused the medical staff to have big concerns about her health and well-being. They informed me that they couldn't let her go home. What?! That wasn't part of the plan. It was clear to me that she needed extra help and care than she was getting but I hadn't envisaged this. She was moved from the home into hospital and quickly declined over the next three months.

Her speech had become confused and unpredictable before going into the home. In hospital she soon became non-verbal and rarely responsive. She adopted a pattern of repeatedly shuffling up and down the corridor of her ward, and needed much more help from the staff to attend to her needs. After a number of weeks she was moved to another hospital which specialised in mental health.

She gradually stopped walking so much, to a point where she just stayed on her bed rocking from side to side. They ended up putting her on a blue mat on the floor for her own safety. The mat looked like the type a gymnast might land on. She lay on the mat and rolled or rocked from side to side. When we visited her all we could do was sit next to her and talk to her without her responding, and try to comfort her as we watched her constantly moving on the mat, on the floor. Just able to put my hand on her arm or head in her discomfort and distress. I fought back my tears during these visits.

As time went on she gradually lost the ability to consume food or drink naturally, and I observed how she got thinner and thinner. The skin on her face became tighter and tighter until it seemed like her teeth were protruding from her mouth or were bigger somehow. It came to the point where the doctors were keeping her alive through tubes which were providing her with the nutrition and water that she needed. She had become very thin, her rocking stopped because she didn't have the strength, and she was put back on a bed again. It was very clear that she was suffering from the grimaces on her face. On one occasion it looked like her eyeballs were coming out of their sockets as she groaned and convulsed in pain. I've never felt more helpless than I did in that moment.

A meeting was set up between us and the relevant hospital staff about her situation. We all went into an office and the door was closed behind us.

"Right", the lead doctor said.

"As you know your mum has been in sharp decline over recent months and is now unable to consume food by herself. We gave her a boost of medication and nutrition which helped, but she has since declined. So, we're at a point now where we could give her another boost but she will decline to where she is now once more, and the cycle will keep repeating. Her organs are failing and she is not comfortable. It's your decision though, and we will give her another boost if that's what you decide to do. We would understand that decision and we would make her as comfortable as we can. So what do you want to do?"

"We should let her go", I said, fully aware of what I was asking the doctors to do. The emotion in my body and behind my eyes made that crystal clear to me.

It was crueller to keep her alive than to allow her suffering to end, but without doubt it was the hardest decision I've ever had to make. To ask the doctors to let my mum die, to let my biggest supporter die was devastating, but I knew it was the right thing to do. Neither my dad nor my brother protested after my instruction was given to the doctors, I think everyone in the room knew it was for the best.

Shortly after that meeting I visited Mum on my own. She couldn't speak but somehow, I hoped that she could hear me and let me know what she wanted. I explained to her what the doctors had asked us.

"If you understand me Mum, can you roll towards me?" She rolled towards me.

"Ok. Mum if you want them to stop your treatment and let you go can you roll away from me?" Mum rolled away from me, and then back to flat on her back again.

"Mum, I'm sorry, I need to be sure that you understand and of what you're telling me. So, if you want them to let you go can you roll away from me again please?"

"Thank you."

Mum rolled away from me for the second time and made her wishes clear. I felt a sense of relief that she agreed with the decision too. It was an altogether different experience visiting Mum after that decision had been made. Knowing that her death was imminent, that these were the final days I would get to see her and spend any time with her. I needed to tell her how I felt before she went but I didn't know how to say it, I wasn't sure I would be able to say it.

So instead, I visited her on my own and I played 'Run' by Leona Lewis to her. The lyrics just seemed to encapsulate what I wanted to say. I looked at her as the song played, crying uncontrollably, now with my body convulsing as I struggled to see her through my tears. She just laid perfectly still and looked into my eyes the whole way through the song, listening intently. Even in her silent stillness I could feel her love for me. As she heard and observed my love for her. She passed away just three months after I dropped her off at the care home, hoping to get her some help. If I had known that, I wouldn't have done it.

Three years later in 2015, we were again sat in the office of a hospital professor that specialised in dementia. I can't imagine how Dad felt when he heard that doctor inform him that he had Alzheimer's too. Knowing what he knew, after watching his wife slowly leave him from that same disease and the horrors that it presented. He broke down and wept, I looked across to him on my right unsure what to do. I put my hand on the top of his back but that felt like a token gesture, and not sufficient for the situation. I was angry and frustrated with him from things that had happened before that meeting, but even so, I really felt for him. I was gutted to hear it confirmed myself. To hear the doctor tell us that my dad would die like my mum, that I had to go through that heartbreaking journey again - slowly and painfully, was horrific for me to hear too.

It had taken at least four years of struggle and frustration to get to that point, to have Dad assessed and achieve a diagnosis. We had been unable to get any help from anywhere until they were able to assess him properly. Achieving the conditions that the doctors needed to be able to assess him had been a weight around my neck, and my brother's too no doubt. I had quit caddying earlier in 2015 because of Dad's situation. On a daily basis I worried about his safety and what might happen to him as he wouldn't listen to me or follow my advice or instruction. He just carried on living his life of self-destruction as I saw it. Living his independence as he saw it. He had little interest in anything since retiring and mum's diagnosis, his only hobby was going to the pub.

I said and did things during that period which I regret to this day, and always will. I was pushed to the very edge of my capacity to cope. Dad was a man of routine which he continued as before but didn't seem to realise how it was affecting me or my brother. It seemed like he didn't care about how it might affect me or my brother, in fact, as if it was our job as his sons to accept his behaviour and look after him. To deal with what his lifestyle and behaviour presented us with. It was very hard to watch as I could see what it was doing to him, he wasn't looking after himself properly at all. He had lost interest in even doing that. I was embarrassed of him at times, as I joined him in the pub. I did so to keep an eye on him and to offer him some company. My eyes and ears would be on hyper alert though, to detect any distain directed towards or about him from other people. I found it very stressful.

This was the same man that I had waited for outside the home dressing room as a four-year-old boy to watch him lead his team out as Port Vale's captain. The professional footballer dad that I looked up at in awe as he walked past me with his team following him down the tiled stairs and out to the pitch to do battle. Hoping that he would ruffle my hair as he went past before I would run up to my seat to watch him play. The man that I wanted to be when I was older.

I was crest fallen at what had become of him, my hero, and the way he was living his life now. This wasn't the same man I had wanted to become, I'm sure this wasn't the man he had wanted to become either. He wasn't the man I knew to be my dad anymore. The grief, depression, alcohol, and Alzheimer's had become him, the habits had become him, and he was now being consumed by them on a daily basis. They were taking him bit by bit. Poisoned by their grip on him, like Superman with kryptonite hanging around his neck. He still looked like him, but my dad wasn't in there anymore, not the dad I knew anyway. Sometimes the dad I recognised fought through to the surface but would be pulled back down again.

We tried to do a detox with him on three occasions, but they failed because the Alzheimer's made it impossible. He couldn't retain the instructions that we gave him and kept forgetting that he wasn't meant to be drinking. We kept trying to remind him and reason with him but without success. It helped to calm him down he said. He was later taken into hospital and as it happened was placed on the same ward where Mum had died. His room was just down the corridor from where she had been. He stayed there for several weeks, and we walked past the room where Mum had taken her last breath each time we visited him.

It had been a long and gruelling process to get him diagnosed, so there was a sense of relief for me when it happened. Relief mixed with heartbreak and the horror of going through again what I had been through with Mum. I wasn't sure that I was going to be able to withstand watching that happen to my other parent too. The first time had been horrendous but this time I knew what was coming and those images appeared in my mind's eye like an old photo album.

How and why could this be happening to us again, and one straight after the other?

When I started my new job as a golf coaching educator, I carried this with me. The death of my mum, the way she had gone, the hole that was left in my life. The ongoing situation of my dad's care and decline. My gran, my mum's mother who lived in Leeds, had also been diagnosed with Alzheimer's - and shortly after Mum's death, was going through the same decline as her daughter. I was her next of kin and dealing with her care and situation too - on top of my dad's.

Each day I carried this out of the front door in the morning - and back through the front door again in the evening. I had not grieved or processed my mum's death really because of my dad's and grandmother's situations. It was the weight of all of this, plus the travelling and demands of my job, the inability to unwind and relax at home, and the lack of sleep, that forced me down onto my knees. To pray in desperation to the God that I didn't believe in.

Chapter 2
Finding My Feet Again

When Dad was first moved into a care home permanently in 2015, I would visit him regularly and take him out. I was also involved in the meetings that took place regarding his care and the outlook going forward. The staff involved with Dad's care decisions spoke to me and my brother as if it was a temporary situation though. That it might still be decided that it would be better for Dad to live at home again. They asked me if I would be his advocate and make the case that he should go home while they performed their assessments on him and his situation. I refused, as I couldn't argue for something I didn't believe was in his best interests. It annoyed me that some other person that I never met did make the case for him as his advocate. How could they do that? Who were they to do that! That's how I felt at the time.

Those assessments both caused me stress and angered me as I waited for their report to come back with their conclusion. We had gone through so much to get to that point and as far as I was concerned it was clearly better for him to be in the care home. He was only going to get worse after all, not better. What on earth were they going on about, and why were they doing that to us? I couldn't understand it as I waited for their findings, believing it could go either way, but each time they came back with what seemed to be an obvious and inevitable verdict. It was better for him to stay where he was. It was a ludicrous process and a complete waste of time in my eyes.

I had found that care homes were not nice places to visit, and they didn't look like nice places to live in either to me, but the residents could seem happier than I expected at times. I hadn't enjoyed going to them previously, and the one that Dad was in was no different. I found it stressful to be in amongst the people that lived in them. I remember one of the senior carers telling us how good it was that me and my brother were visiting Dad regularly because plenty of relatives don't. I felt it was only right that I did visit and take him out as he was my dad, and he had done plenty for me. I was only doing what I was meant to be doing in that situation.

Regrettably though, after I started my new job as a golf lecturer in September 2016, I did become one of those relatives that didn't visit much for quite a long period of time. I hadn't been working when he first went into the home and then became a full-time student, so I had the energy and capacity to regularly visit and take him out. After about one year or so in my new job, that changed. If there was an issue of any kind I was there, but my rate of visiting him and taking him out fell away. There was a good six-month period where I didn't see him much at all, maybe longer. It pains me to write it but that's what happened. I just didn't have the energy or will to go. I was too tired and too depressed, too sad and frustrated that I was still having to deal with a parent and grandparent with Alzheimer's. With work, the commute, and no real respite at home I was really struggling with my mental health, and both my dad and my gran were getting worse.

Leading up to this period where I stopped visiting as much, the weekends were when I had hoped to recover from my week at work. I found it difficult to do though, because my weekends involved looking after my dad. I would pick him up from the home, and take him to watch my brother play football on a Saturday and Sunday, as he loved watching him play. It wasn't just about watching the matches though, there was the socialising before and after the game too and then taking him back to the home again. Both games would take up about five hours all in all.

I found it stressful because I was on edge about what Dad might do at any time, or what I might have to do. He had also developed a tremor in his right hand which could be very noticeable. I think we were both self-conscious about it. He would hold his right wrist with his left hand to reduce the shaking, but still he struggled to just take a drink out of a glass or cup. It was hard to watch. I stressed about how other people would behave around him and how they might treat him. So often people can be cruel to a perceived easy target like he was. I'd seen that lots of times through my life; indeed I'd been that easy target myself.

As we stood at the side of the pitch, he would sometimes ask me why he was in a home and what was wrong with him. He had been asking me these questions since he went into the home, which he objected to when it happened. I wasn't sure how to answer. Tell him the truth and upset him or don't tell him the truth and leave him confused or lied to? Neither was a good option. I asked him if he remembered what the doctor had said to him, which usually he remembered and that seemed to settle it for him. I watched his face and body language to look for signs of sadness or stress, but he was usually ok. It was good for Dad to be out in the world and doing something that stimulated him, but it frustrated me too. My brother was doing what he wanted to do and would be doing anyway regardless, whereas I probably wouldn't have been there if it wasn't for taking Dad. If I didn't take him and look after him though, he would have been stuck in the home. I felt obligated to take him as his son, but my lack of autonomy frustrated me.

I was feeling tired and stressed seven days per week and couldn't find a way to relax and unwind. I developed a mind-set where my mind's eye was always looking round the corner for the next wave of distress, pain and grief to come crashing towards it.

In early 2017, I went back to Matt's house, a good mate of mine, after a night out drinking with our mates. We opened another can and were just talking about whatever, then the topic of my dad came up. Suddenly a wave of emotion crashed into me as I told him about the latest situation. I broke down and told him, with despair in my voice,

"I can't do it, I can't watch that again, I can't watch that again, I can't watch my other parent die like that again, I can't, I can't, I can't do it."

My body shook as I cried with my hands over my face supporting the weight of my head and despair. Matt became choked up himself, which was very unlike him, and through his own emotions he tried to encourage me that I could do it and would get through it.

"You can, you can do this mate, you'll get through this. We'll help you."

It was shortly after that conversation that I found myself, as described at the start of the book, down on my knees praying to the God I didn't believe in. Weeks after I said that prayer it was Matt that messaged me and asked me if I fancied going to Parkrun on Saturday morning with him. I had no idea what it was apart from obviously being about going for a run. I declined the offer at first, I was too depressed and low to go. He asked me again though the following week and I agreed, I had recognised that I was going to need to do something to help myself. I needed to have different thoughts and activities if I was going to climb out of the hole that I was in.

That Saturday morning I struggled out of bed and got my running gear on. I was not in good shape or fitness to say the least, certainly not compared to my history as a footballer, which I had stopped playing ten years earlier. I had become a stranger to exercise and had developed a coping strategy of taking solace in alcohol and a poor diet. Using short term gratification to remove me from my depression and struggles. I just wanted the world, and life, to leave me alone for a while. The beer and bad food allowed me to escape from it for a period of time, brief as it was. This approach did little for my mental state overall though.

I wasn't sure what I'd let myself in for as I sat in the front passenger seat of his car. We arrived at the park, where the run was, and made our way up the hill towards the start line. It was a beautiful park located in the middle of houses and flats. As we walked through it there were cones lined up to mark the track for the run, there was a serene scenic lake and grass and trees, a canal that we crossed over and playgrounds for children to play on. It was beautiful. Coming from the forest of concrete that surrounded it I didn't expect to arrive in such beautiful and natural surroundings.

As we crossed over the canal, I saw the bandstand in the middle of a landscaped garden setting. The railing of the bandstand had lots of jackets, tops, bags and other belongings hanging over it, and there were people everywhere. They were walking to the start line and bandstand from all directions, they were congregating in groups chatting and laughing, and jogging around or stretching to warm up. I had a history of pulling my tight muscles, so I started my own warm up too and realised just how tight and unfit my muscles had become.

As I moved my Chinese take-away(s), pizzas, chocolate and beer into a jogging motion I could see and feel an energy around me which was different. I hadn't felt it anywhere else. We lined up behind the start line just before 9am and listened to the organiser explain how it was to work. They asked if there were any first timers that morning and I, among others, put my hand up. Then the rest of the runners cheered and clapped us, about three hundred of them. I felt myself get slightly taller when they applauded me for just turning up for the first time. They then celebrated other peoples' milestones for how many times they had turned up. Fifty, one hundred and more.

We were given the health and safety briefing and then the organiser counted down.

"Five, four, three, two, one, go!"

Off I went on the five-kilometre run jogging alongside Matt. I wasn't able to stay with him for long though. The run was a big struggle for me, but I enjoyed the feeling of my body moving and the blood pumping through my veins again like I'd felt before, but not for some time. The route was hard because of the setting of the park on a big hill so there were several sections where I had to drag those takeaways and beers up the hill. But I kept going and kept trotting on.

I was, in my mind, running terribly, but as I went round the route there were people that I had never met clapping me and encouraging me onwards. It was both confusing and invigorating at the same time. Other runners were going past me and telling me to keep going or saying well done, 'well done for being crap' I thought; it still felt good though. This was not how people usually behaved - this was not how they usually treated me anyway. Although I was running through treacle, those other people gave me energy.

The end of the run involved winding around the lake at the bottom of the park and then running up a slight incline before arriving at the foot of a steep hill which crossed back over the canal. I was struggling to keep my legs moving during this stretch. It was deceiving because in my mind I believed that I was getting close to the finish, but it was taking quite a while to get around the lake. As I made my way along the incline on the other side of the lake, I saw that there was a woman of about sixty years old up ahead. My ego suddenly appeared on my shoulder and whispered,

"You can't let her beat you Mart, that would be embarrassing".

So, I dug deep and increased my pace - I caught up with her too and overtook her just before the turn left to go up the steep hill.

Now I needed to push on up the hill and stay in front of her. I mauled my body up the hill, giving it everything I had. It seemed to go on and on, each step taking extra effort to lift my feet above the stony path, and it seemed to take ages to reach the top where the ground levelled out again. The photographer stationed at the top took a photo of my gurning red face with my mouth desperately trying to find more oxygen. Thanks. Finally, I made it, the hard part was done and now I just needed to jog round the corner to the left and on to the finish line on the flat again.

I made my way round the bend with my ego intact. Then that sixty-year-old woman casually appeared next to me and jogged on past me again. The one that I couldn't lose to. "Well done keep going" she said with a cheery voice. I panted back to her. She started to pull away from me little by little, I begged my legs to respond and catch her again, but their orange light was on, there was barely any fuel in the tank. Just fumes. I tried to pump my arms and stay with her, but it was over, and I watched her slowly get smaller. All I could do was keep going as best I could. When I got to the finish line people were clapping me in and telling me well done. It was the first taste of something good and encouraging that I had experienced for a long time.

After the run there was a hall in a church at the bottom end of the park, which was opened for those from Parkrun to go to afterwards. Many of the runners and organisers went in for refreshments, we just had to donate a pound or two. I hoped I had just donated a couple of pounds of lard at least, during the run. Another mate of ours, John, was there with some of his family so we sat around a table chatting with our coffees and toast. I felt some of my coils unwind slightly and some of my stress lift from my body. It was rare to experience such a positive sense of community and camaraderie. Complete strangers encouraging and supporting me. I needed to do this again.

The following Saturday Matt picked me up again and I enjoyed the encouraging and supportive atmosphere once more. I gained a sense of achievement from completing the run, then went to the church for coffee again. The coffee was really nice too; the proper filter sort. John and his family went to the church on a Sunday too, had done for several years, so he knew people that would be in the church. In fact, it was his sister and brother in-laws that ran the church café after Parkrun.

I got to know his wife, Naomi, and their children better as the weeks went by. The children were young so they would be at their grandparents, who lived right next to the church, while their parents did the run. Naomi's dad had been the pastor at the church for decades before recently retiring, and John and Naomi had met in the church as teenagers. So, the children and grandparents came into the church from next door after the run.

They had (still do) three children; Seb, Jude and Isla - Jude could be described as disabled because of his inability to talk and from being physically and mentally underdeveloped. I knew of him, but I'd not met him, or his siblings and Mum before. When I first met Jude, I was sympathetic and felt sorry for him because of his situation. I quickly learned though, that he was one of the happiest people I'd ever met. He would celebrate and cheer for the simplest of things. Naomi would tell him for example, with Makaton sign language, that they were having pizza for dinner, and he would throw his hands up in the air with joy and jump up and down with a big smile on his face. I watched him, laughing myself, and wished that I could be more like him. Someone that celebrated small things like they were big things, someone with that kind of gratitude and joy for life.

The church was more like a school hall than a traditional church. Jude loved football and would play with a sponge football in his own imagination, scoring goals against the wall and then running off and sliding on his knees in celebration. When other children, without his challenges, were playing football he would just join in without hesitation, which really struck me as I watched and thought of my own shyness. He really left an impression on me with how joyful and enthusiastic he was despite, what appeared to me to be, his problems and issues. It was like he didn't recognise them, and that was helping to create his bliss as I observed with envy. I couldn't help but self-reflect and feel a little guilty over my mindset and attitude towards my own situation. Things that he didn't have or couldn't do, I took for granted, but he was much happier than me.

As the weeks went on, I slowly got fitter and improved my times for the run. I got my barcode which they create for each runner and then scan at the end of the run. I became keen to see what my time was on their website each week. We tended to have the same group of us around the same table which helped me to become more comfortable in the church cafe afterwards as we waited for our times.

I started to join in with Jude when he played football on his own. He would excitedly go in goal and then commentate with his noises of enthusiasm as I took shots. Or I would go in goal and when he scored, he would run off and celebrate like Harry Kane, his favourite footballer. I laughed watching him and was happy to let him score as subtly as I could. John's other son, Seb, was slightly older and a keen footballer too. It soon developed into me playing football with him as well, and then John also. Particularly as the church hall became quiet again after people had left. The four of us would play keep-ball where one of us was in the middle until we intercepted the ball.

The run and encouragement, followed by the coffee and toast, and conversations which were free from threat or concern for me were a real tonic. To join hundreds of people that just supported and encouraged each other, and celebrated people for just turning up was uplifting. Then I joined friends for coffee and played football with Seb, helping him with his game, and Jude - who looked to me like he had everything against him, but behaved like everything was going for him. He was inspiring for me.

As the weeks went by, I got that little bit fitter and my ambition to reduce my time grew that little bit more. I felt better from the regular exercise and improved fitness, and I felt better from being part of that small community. After completing the run, I felt like I deserved that coffee and toast, and to sit down for those chats with friends. I enjoyed the conversations and each week watched Jude do what he loved with joy, and celebrate the smallest and simplest of things like he had just won a holiday to Disneyland.

I continued to struggle in my own world. Those Saturday mornings though, they were the highlight of my week. I arrived curled inwards and heavy, but left feeling taller and more capable of coping with my life and situation for one more week. It was a matter of choice and perspective. I needed to see the things to be grateful for and start to celebrate the small things more, just like Jude did.

Chapter 3

The Exploration Begins

The church hall was a rectangular shape where it was clearly wider than it was long, and the entrance was from the side of the bottom right corner while the kitchen was adjacent to the top right corner. It had a wooden polished floor which was partly covered with temporary tables and grey plastic chairs down the right side and across the bottom with some space left for children to play in. There were also two or three tables laid out in a line, at a right angle to the kitchen hatch and just to the left of it, where the mugs and urns were put out for us to help ourselves from. There was always a small wicker basket next to them for us to make our small donation of a pound or two, a very reasonable deal.

I wearily walked in, took my trainers off as we had to and put them on the mat provided for everyone, then went and sat at the usual table, which was the one closest to the coffee urns and the hatch where the food was served. We weren't daft, it was a perk of going in early and knowing the organisers. It's all about who you know. I was sat on the far side of the table with my back to the kitchen and facing towards the entrance to the church hall. I lifted my mug to my mouth and took a sip of my coffee, and as I did so a blonde woman, who looked about my age, eased her way into the cafe. I'd never seen her before, and I watched her as she slowly made her way into the hall.

It turned out that John and Naomi knew her from church and invited her to join us. So, we were introduced, and we started chatting with Karen as we got to know her more. The two of us who didn't know her bounced off each other as we made jokes and took the mick out of her a bit, in a playful way. Me particularly as I was attracted to her. Karen became a regular part of our group from then on and so we got to know her more as the weeks went on. She was quietly spoken and seemed to be an introverted person like me. This all helped me to feel more comfortable with her as we spoke.

One week I was talking with her, and I found myself telling her my back story of where I was coming from and what I was trying to recover from. I knew that it was a sad story, which was why I usually kept it to myself so that I didn't bring people down with me, as I knew that people didn't want that from me. I was conscious of doing that to her as I spoke. I didn't consider myself good at speaking with women but surely that was the opposite of what I needed to do to get her interested. Depressing her was not the ticket to getting a date with her, I was sure. She had asked though, and so I gave her an honest answer and surprisingly she seemed to be interested by my story, and empathetic to what I had been through and was still going through.

The next week we were talking again, and Karen was telling me that she really wanted to go to the cinema to watch a film that was out. She said it in a way that made me think that she was asking me if I wanted to go with her, but without actually saying it. 'Is she asking me out?' I thought. 'No, she can't be. It seems that way though.' There was surely no way that my depressing story had led to her covertly asking me out. So, I let it pass and didn't risk finding out for sure. At home later I mulled it over further, going round in mental circles. Finally, I decided that I didn't want to miss out from not being brave enough to say something, so I messaged her on social media. She admitted that she was asking me to go with her. Which was good news, but at the same time it caused me some concern.

I did not relish the pressure of impressing her. After all I was a thirty-seven-year-old man and still living in the family home, whereas she was a fully grown adult woman living in her house with her two kids. I hadn't come close to any of that. I obviously did something right though when we went to watch the film, and thereafter, because the dates continued and we spoke more and more via messaging.

Then she informed me that she couldn't start a relationship with me because I wasn't a Christian. Her religion strongly advised that she should only enter into a relationship with another Christian so that she wouldn't get pulled away from her faith. I made an argument against that idea in an attempt to convince her otherwise, but I got nowhere with it. She stuck firmly to her beliefs despite my well thought out protests and counter-arguments. Why couldn't she just compromise a bit like I was prepared to do? Meet me halfway.

I liked her though, and I had been curious about God for a long time, going back to childhood in fact. There had been several occasions where I had thought about looking into it more and going to a church but had never bothered. Given that fact, I decided that now was the time to investigate it properly. I didn't want to miss out on the relationship through arrogance or ignorance. So, I started to go to the church on Sunday mornings as well as Saturday mornings.

I was apprehensive on the first Sunday morning. I felt like I was going to somebody else's party, and I hadn't been formally invited. I walked into the church just before it was due to start so that I could avoid too much social discomfort in a hall full of strangers. I said hello as briefly as politeness would allow and then intently looked for a seat. Thankfully a friendly old man guided me to where there was a spare seat at the back of the hall, which suited me fine.

The church was full of people, but they were nearly all facing away from me towards the front, which helped me to relax more because they couldn't see me. I looked for Karen and saw that she was in the family section towards the spot where we sat on a Saturday morning. John and his family were in that section too over to the right side of the church. I felt more at ease knowing some of the people there.

The pastor walked to the front and said with a smile, "Good morning everyone, my name is James and I am a pastor here at this church. You are all very welcome".

He said a few announcements and then teed up the first song. People out of the audience walked to the front and stood by microphones or got ready to play an instrument, including James. Everyone looked up at the screens hanging high on the wall at the front of the church to read the lyrics that they should sing as the music started. It was no shock to me that the three songs that were then sung were about Jesus and God. It felt a bit awkward for me to sing those words when I didn't believe them or mean them. I felt like I was lying. I did sing along though, not exactly with gusto, but I did sing as it was the polite thing to do.

After the songs James put his bass guitar down and returned to front and centre. He then eased his way into his sermon which was of course about Jesus and God some more, but I was impressed by it because I was still able to take a good practical message from it for how I could live better. Even though I didn't believe in God or Jesus. That gave me further encouragement to go again. It was also quite a positive experience, being amongst a group who were on the same side and supportive of each other. Like Saturday mornings in a way.

Over several weeks and months, I went to the Sunday services and investigated the Christian religion, or faith as they called it. I heard them preach over the weeks about how God loves us all, that he wants us all to be with him in heaven for eternity. However, if we didn't declare that we were following him and that we loved him then we would end up in Hell for eternity instead. How could God love us, but he was willing to send us to Hell? I took this as being like someone holding a gun to my head and telling me that I needed to love them to live. It didn't seem right to me and made me more resistant and even more convinced that it was all nonsense. How could it be my free will that chose to follow him in those circumstances?

I read books and articles on the subject by those for and against Christianity. I watched numerous debates on YouTube between Christians and atheists. Every one of them that I watched I would have given the victory to the atheist. They spoke from science and the discoveries that we have made and can prove, as well as the things from the Bible that science had disproven in their view. There was logic and reasoning behind their arguments whereas the Christians just had the Bible. The ancient book that I couldn't be sure was true.

That was one of my biggest issues in terms of believing in God and Jesus. The Bible. I couldn't believe the source itself; it made claims that seemed ludicrous, it was written who knows when by who knows who, and we knew so much more now than the authors did back then. The Bible was primitive and outdated. As the atheists pointed out, science had moved us beyond the Bible and made it redundant. We had looked into the universe deeper than ever and had gone beyond the claims of the Bible. I watched the prominent atheists time and time again tear through the Christian argument. When the pastors or others at the church referred to the Bible to make their arguments for Christianity, they had lost me already because I had no faith in it.

I carried on a complex and on-off relationship with Karen, while I explored the Christian faith. My going to church and exploring the Christian faith was why the relationship had been able to continue at all in some form. I had signed up for a course for people like me to explore Christianity, but by the time it was due to start I felt that I had already made my mind up. It didn't make sense to me and so I couldn't commit to it. I felt it probably pointless to go to the course with the decision already made, but I decided to go anyway. It would be the final act of my investigation before calling it a day and moving on. I would just go and take what I could from it.

The 'Christianity Explored' course, ran by Steve, the other pastor at the church, centred around the book of Mark. To begin with there were six or seven of us, but as the weeks went on the number reduced to three of us that were consistently there each week. I was a pain in the neck for Steve as I asked him lots of questions, challenging what was being said week after week. Credit to him though, he kept answering my questions and didn't appear to become exasperated with me. It just didn't make sense to me. There were too many holes and contradictions in it, too many things which just seemed to be ridiculous or didn't add up.

I was a man that loved science and physics. I had read and watched a lot on physics from people like Einstein, Hawking and Neil Degrasse Tyson and his panel discussions. I was in the science camp and wasn't budging for this rubbish. After about six weeks of the course, I explained to Steve and the others that I just wasn't having it. It just didn't make sense to me, and I couldn't connect the dots. How could I trust a book from so long ago that made such outlandish claims with no way of knowing if it was true. There was no way of proving that God existed, not like science had proven the existence of the Higgs Boson particle for example.

The Bible claimed that God had been amongst his people thousands of years ago and spoke to people from the sky, but there was no report of that happening now. No reports of anything like that happening in recent decades or centuries. Then there was the 'love me or else' demand that God made of us. That didn't get my respect.

After listening to me describe my disbelief and resistance to the Christian faith one of the women there suggested that instead of just trying to make sense of it academically and intellectually, I should try doing it. Try living it out in some way and see what happens. It was an intriguing idea, and to my mind, the last stone that was left unturned. Later that night

I lay in my bed, closed my eyes and truly prayed to God for the second time in my life. I spoke into the air my thoughts, doubts and concerns, my wants and needs. I had learned by now to sign off and end the prayer with

"In Jesus' name, Amen."

After I finished, I noticed a calmness and peace that had come over me. Then I eventually went to sleep. When I got out of bed for work the next morning, that peace was still with me. As I drove to work, I was tired as normal, but felt a little more peaceful and lighter somehow.

However, despite the clear difference that I had experienced from praying, my prior concerns and struggles didn't just suddenly leave me. I still struggled to accept the foundational principles of the Christian faith. Why did God create that serpent which he knew would corrupt Adam and Eve? What was the point of creating the Earth and humanity but then have to send your own son down to suffer and die in order to make up for their failings? Which only started because of the demonic serpent that you created and put on the Earth in the first place?

All the talk of sin too, and that the only way was to follow Jesus. Every week, follow Jesus, follow Jesus, God loves you, Jesus died for you. I couldn't see, hear or touch either of them though. They were just an idea to me, characters from an ancient book which could easily be fiction, like so many books. I considered myself to be a relatively intelligent guy and I was not going to fall for this. Praying to God and Jesus was doing something positive for me though, and therein lied the tension that I wrestled with.

Chapter 4
A Night of Testimony

Karen and I went to her auntie's church one Sunday morning. It was in a brick building that looked more like a factory than a church. Upstairs there was a big open room with a stage set up in one section and chairs set up facing the stage. There weren't that many chairs set out and not so many people listening to the preacher on the stage either, maybe forty people. It soon became clear to me that this was a different type of church to the one we normally went to. There were people calling out from the audience and there was a big American bloke on the stage preaching who kept repeating slogans all the time.

"Amen",

"Hallelujah" the audience would respond. The preacher had a white towel in one hand and a microphone in the other. He was interesting to listen to and very energetic in his style of preaching, which was reciprocated from the audience. He was doing a tour of churches in the UK to promote his new book, which was an eye opener for me. How can a preacher go round looking to profit from what they preach? The book has already been written hasn't it? I realised afterwards though, that his book was about how to practice your faith and offered insights and interpretations from the Bible. I was a little sceptical to be honest as it seemed like it might be more about the show and book sales than preaching. That was why he used so many catchy slogans perhaps?

At the end of his talk though, he invited people to go to the front if they hadn't said the prayer that commits their life to Jesus. By this point I was more knowledgeable and experienced about and in the Christian faith. I wouldn't say that I had been convinced yet though. When he asked, I awkwardly smiled and pondered the invitation, then Karen asked me if I was going up, and I decided to go to the front. What harm could it do?

The preacher led us through the prayer, and we repeated each portion after him. The room was filled with positive energy and excitement. I felt it fill my body as I spoke out the prayer that proclaimed my faith in God and Jesus. I was filled with joy and excitement and a smile spread across my face. I walked back to my seat feeling like a different person, like a new person, like my life had just started. I felt clean on the inside.

The irony was that Karen and I split up again shortly after that Sunday. It was a bit awkward to go to the same church as her and her kids, but I had to keep going for my growing relationship with God. That insane relationship with something that I couldn't see or hear - but still it felt like we were communicating somehow. The pastors spoke of God as a person, but I viewed God as energy. Energy I could sense and feel. Energy that was slowly lifting the heavy iron suit that had built up on me over time.

It felt like I was being unburdened and lightened from the inside. I drove to the church one Sunday and came to a stop at some traffic lights, when I had a strange feeling in my chest. It was like there was something lodged in my airway that was slowly moving upwards, like it was gradually being pulled out. What I felt moving though was not a physical thing, it was like a ball of energy that was making that area feel heavier than it was. I felt it move upwards inch by inch, at first my mouth was closed but as I felt it rising, I opened my mouth to let it out. I could feel that it was lighter now where it had moved from, and felt whatever it was leave through my mouth. It was crazy, I can't explain what it was, all I knew at the time was I felt better afterwards.

I understood more and was much more open to what the Bible said by this point, but I was still struggling with it. What I really wanted to hear was people's stories about how becoming a Christian and being a Christian had played out in their lives. I wanted to listen to stories which I could relate to, that would make this seem more real and current. Then my opportunity arrived. Our church was to have a night of testimony.

I was excited as I drove to church that Sunday evening. I couldn't wait to finally hear about other peoples' experiences and what had happened in their lives as Christians. This would hopefully bring it off the pages of the Bible and bring it into a more contemporary reality. These stories would be closer to me, closer in time and closer in context, which would help me to feel like it was more tangible and relatable.

I walked into the church about fifteen minutes before it was due to start, which was very early for me, and took a seat in the second row, over to the left side. There were about fifty chairs laid out in a semi-circle, which was far fewer than for the morning service. I was a little nervous that people wouldn't turn up for me to listen to. The more people there were filling those seats the better the odds were of filling the time allotted with peoples' stories. I monitored the room as the time moved towards six thirty, when we were due to start.

Thankfully people did turn up and most of the seats were supporting somebody. There was a microphone set up at the front of the church on its own, front and centre, waiting for people to tell their stories. Like an open mic night. James walked over to the mic and welcomed everyone to the church for the night of testimony, and then introduced a song for us all to sing. For some reason that surprised me, I was so focussed on the story telling part I guess, I didn't expect the singing first.

The song that we started to sing was about gratitude to God for all that he had done for us. A fitting choice for the night. As I sang, I also thought about what God had done for me. I became overwhelmed with emotion and my eyes pooled with tears of thankfulness. The difference between where I had come from to where I was as I stood there singing was massive. By no means complete, by no means free from the struggle and grief, but certainly a different person living in a different world. Not that the world had changed much, it was my view of my world that had changed.

As the song continued, I became alarmed because I was getting a sense that I was meant to walk to that lonely microphone and tell my story. I hadn't gone to tell my story though, that wasn't the plan; I was there to listen to others. To become more convinced of this way of life and faith through the real testimonies of others already living that life. Those with more experience and knowledge than me on the subject.

James asked his audience for who was going to go up and tell their testimony. Nobody wanted to go first though. There was no response as people looked around at each other hoping to see somebody else stand up or raise their hand. Nobody did. James asked again. Thankfully a lady stood up and walked to the front. Phew, I was worried that I wouldn't get to hear a testimony for a second there. I listened with intent, but it was a Bible centred one which referred to scripture and certain verses. That wasn't what I was after, I wanted to hear life stories. Then others went up and told of how God had seen them through difficult times. One lad told of how he had no job, no money and couldn't pay his rent but then God delivered him a job by unusual means. A young woman told of how she couldn't sense God in her life at all and how distressing and upsetting it had been for her.

As I sat and listened, I felt the sense that I was meant to tell my story grow. I kept checking the time as I listened to others. The night was to finish at seven-thirty. I looked at the doors that served as the entrance and exit from the church. I checked my watch. I looked at James, I looked at the person telling their story. I felt like I was being told not to walk back through those doors without giving my testimony. But I really didn't want to do that.

It got to 7.20pm, and James asked for the last person to go up and give their testimony. I looked around the room, but nobody moved. I felt an overwhelming pressure to tell my story before I left and so I felt compelled to do it. I put my hand up, nerves rushed into all parts of my body, and I could feel myself starting to shake internally. I asked if it was ok to tell more of a life story. James said that was ok – which, if I am honest was a slight disappointment. Then I stood up and walked to the microphone.

When I arrived at the mic and faced the room, I stood silently looking at the faces in front of me for a moment as I processed my situation. I sheepishly started to speak, not really knowing how I was going to form my story. Where to begin? I was still working that out as I stood at the mic. A vague plan quickly formed in my mind, and I started, shakily, my voice just about managing to squeeze through the cracks in my fear. As I spoke, I became emotional, great. It was a slow, winding and emotional testimony. The very type of testimony that I had wanted to hear from somebody else. Instead, I heard it from my own mouth. After I had finished speaking the audience applauded me and James put his hand on my shoulder then prayed for me.

I could walk back out of the church knowing that I had done as I was told to. I had told my story. I realise that these words could make me sound like I had lost my mind. What I am talking of is not another voice, or a vision, I am talking of a sense in my body as a whole. A gut feeling you might say; that I was meant to tell my story and I better not leave without doing so. So I did. Several of the audience came up to me afterwards and thanked me individually for doing so. It was very powerful they said.

As I walked out of the church, I felt that little bit lighter again. I felt grateful, but also a little apprehensive of what the other people had thought of my long, sobbing story. However, no matter what those in the audience had thought, in the days that followed I continued to feel that gratitude, and a sense of joy.

Despite still living my troubled and grief-stricken existence, I found that releasing that emotion and hearing myself tell my story of what God had (and was) still doing in my life, had given me great encouragement. I left the church that night with a stronger connection with Christianity, and God, but not in the way that I had anticipated. It wasn't from listening to other peoples' stories. It was from re-living and listening to mine.

Chapter 5
Learning Who I Am

About six months into my time as a golf lecturer, which would also have been in the Spring of 2017, I performed a Google search for why I was falling asleep at my computer. It had been concerning me how long I was taking to complete my tasks, and I worried that my bosses may start to notice it and question my work ethic or ability to do the job. The reading required was like swimming through treacle for me. I could feel myself becoming more and more tired as I read, until I realised that my head had slumped forward, and my eyes had closed, not good.

At first, I thought it was due to the lack of sleep at night, the travelling, and the general fatigue I was experiencing from my life. However, I came to believe that there was more to it than that. Hence the decision to do the classic Google search, and hope I didn't find out that I had a serious illness. The results of the search brought up numerous results which all said the same thing. Dyslexia. Eh? How could I have got to 37 years old and not know that I could be dyslexic? My generation weren't picked up for that type of thing at school though like they are now, so it could be possible. It could have gone undetected, frustrating as that might turn out to be.

An online assessment suggested that I might be dyslexic too, which convinced me to pursue a formal assessment for dyslexia. So I booked an appointment and paid the £500 fee. At the end of a two hour long assessment the psychologist told me that she was on the fence about my situation. The results leant towards dyslexia, but she didn't believe them to be conclusive and said that she would need more time to consider my case further. I was willing her to diagnose me, but I guess she ended up on the side of caution with her verdict that I wasn't dyslexic, which was frustrating for me.

I was left still void of a diagnosis to tell my employers. The report I was sent did offer a form of explanation for my struggles though, and recommendations for how to manage them. Interestingly, there was also a suggestion that I look into a condition called Irlen Syndrome. Irlen what? I'd never heard of it. My research informed me that it was a struggle of the brain to process light coming into the eyes which caused stress and fatigue in the brain because of the extra work it had to do compared with the norm. Maybe that was why I was becoming so tired at the computer and struggling to sleep at night because of the struggle of my brain to calm down again at the end of the day? So I paid the fee to be assessed for Irlen Syndrome too.

After the interview process, the assessor concluded that it was very likely that I did have Irlen Syndrome and that we should carry on to the next stage. She explained to me that people with Irlen Syndrome are particularly sensitive to certain colours from the spectrum of light. That blew my mind a little. They also have colours which are more calming for them too, mine turned out to be blue. Which made sense thinking of my wardrobe. I then tried numerous different coloured filters, shaped like typical lenses for glasses, over my eyes and focussed on the effects they had on me. I could literally feel the effort and tension increase from some colours, as the blood rushed up into my head and my shoulders and body tensed up.

When I held the optimal filters in front of my eyes, I felt the blood drain from my head and my shoulders drop. I became a little dizzy for a moment from the blood rush, but it felt like my head and body breathed a big sigh of relief at the same time. The relaxation that came over me was profound, as I discovered the thing that I had been missing all my life but didn't know it. It brought an intense sense of relief.

It was mystifying really; how could those filters make such a difference? Why had I never heard of Irlen Syndrome? I couldn't help but reflect on my life and how this could have influenced it. The colour found to give me the most trouble was green, which was a revelation for me because I had spent a large portion of my professional life working on top of that colour. As a young professional footballer, and a professional golf caddie particularly I had been working on grass. Was this part of the struggle that I went through as a young footballer at Aston Villa? Was this why I was so exhausted after caddying for a round of golf, but still struggled to sleep? Maybe, I could give myself more of a break for why I didn't have a career as a footballer like my dad did? Maybe I could stop believing that I let my dad and myself down - that I failed my potential? There could be a reasonable explanation.

While the new glasses and filters did make a positive difference, I still got to a point in my job as a golf lecturer where I felt I needed to leave. With what had happened to my parents I had decided not to put a job over my health. It was a tough decision though, because I still remembered when I first got the job and felt like I had landed my dream job. I also wasn't sure what I might do instead. I consoled myself by the fact that it wasn't the only job in the world and that I should be able to get another one somewhere. I believed strongly in this principle and so I started to really look for another job. I had been looking at job pages for quite a while, but now I was looking with a real intent of actually applying for new employment.

I was hoping to find one that was considered to be a 'good job' that would become a 'good career'. A job that would be respected by other people and would bring me a 'good' salary and pension all being well. It just so happened at that time that there was a big recruitment drive by the police for

20,000 new officers. I had never seen myself as a policeman and I can't say that I did at that time either, but it did fit the mould that I was looking to fill and was the best option available to me at the time. So I applied. The process for joining the police would be long and arduous though. I started with stage one of filling out the paperwork and sent it to them, and included my diagnosis of Irlen Syndrome.

I carried on in my current job as a golf lecturer, knowing that I was planning to leave. It helped in a way to deal with my frustrations because I knew that I didn't need those things to change anymore. I was going to be the change myself, which brought more of a sense of control I guess. I received news from the police that I had passed through the paperwork stage and was now through to stage two. The assessment centre, so far so good.

By this time I was now the subject lead on the Golf Coaching courses at work after being promoted, which included lecturing and assessing students for the full-time degree that we offered through a local university. My colleague, who oversaw the full-time degree, informed me, as a subject leader, that the open day for that programme would be on Friday 13th of the next month. It struck me that it would be on that date because of the superstition of bad luck associated with Friday 13th in the UK. Through my lifetime it had always been identified as an unlucky date and day combination, where bad things tended to happen. Therefore, people would usually avoid it when organising something, or hope to get through the day unscathed when it arrived. Was he asking for trouble by going with that date I wondered? He obviously didn't believe in the superstition around it and wasn't concerned anyway.

Shortly after that news, in the weeks following, my brother and I took Dad to watch a Stoke City home game. We only decided to do it that morning. He loved football and we thought taking him to a local professional match would be a good afternoon out for us to spend with him. We were in the main stand behind the dugouts and were high up towards the top which gave us a good view. It did not go unnoticed for me though as I went to pull my seat down that it had the number 13 on it. That was two in relatively quick succession. Nothing more than an amusing coincidence though.

For my next assessment with the police, I had been invited to a venue in Coventry. So, I drove down to the assessment centre, making sure that I was there before the 13:30 start time. As I parked up at the venue, I saw that the clock in my car said 13:00. I then went in and was met by one of the staff who was handing out lanyards with candidate numbers on. I was given number 13. This was getting my attention now, there was a pattern forming.

We were assessed in various ways for about five hours, and it was tough! They tested our ability to take in information quickly and then act on it in live role plays. We were assessed on our ability to listen to a person's story and then retell it as accurately as possible. There was a maths assessment and a language assessment as well as an interview. I nearly gave up in the assessment where we watched a video and had to retell the story. I became lost and demoralised, in the past I would have given up through frustration, but for some reason I went again that day. When I walked back out of the assessment centre to my car, I felt mentally shattered and pleased it was all over.

Shortly after that assessment I went to the church holiday. I'd never been before but John told me that it was usually a good week. It was in the middle of the countryside. I drove down the long narrow driveway, which would just about fit two cars. Either side of me were fields with cows grazing or looking on as I drove past. I drove through some woodland and past the tennis courts, then I caught sight of the large stately home looking building with its many windows. There was a circular lawn in front of the main entrance, I could imagine horse-drawn carriages riding around it and pulling up in front of the big front door. I carried on around to the side of the building to the main car park. It was late afternoon when I arrived and most of the group were already there, if not all of them.

I walked into the grand building with my small suitcase, not knowing where to go. Thankfully I bumped into people from church who pointed me down the corridor to where the staff would be in the shop/office. I introduced myself to the lady and checked in for the week. I was given the key to the room for my stay, and my eyes fixated on the key in wonder as it sat in my palm. There it was again – room 13.

My room was basic as the cost had suggested it would be, but it would do. I unpacked my stuff and then went back down to join the large group from the church for dinner. I was a little nervous as I made my way down the stairs and walked through the doorway to the large dining room. There were about six rows of large tables sat horizontally on both sides of the room with an aisle through the middle, each table surrounded by people as far as I could tell. At the far end, beyond the people, was the food laid out like a buffet, so it would be difficult to get food unnoticed.

I looked around the room scanning for threats and opportunities, for people that I would feel more uncomfortable or comfortable sitting with. Looking for somewhere to sit where I wouldn't feel too anxious and self-conscious. The room was full of families and groups of people that knew each other well. I felt awkward as I looked around, and a little overwhelmed by the number of people in there and the noise they were making which bounced around the room. Thankfully I saw John and Naomi and was invited to join them and their children, which was a big relief. I was happy to sit with them, so my mind and body calmed down again.

After dinner I didn't fancy hanging around in one of the lounges or sitting rooms with people I didn't really know - I felt too awkward to do that, so I retreated to the safety of my room to chill out on my own. I had a Bible app on my phone which offered reading plans on certain topics or parts of the Bible. At that time, the plan that I was reading was going through the book of 1 Corinthians. I was enjoying it too. So, when I got up to my room, I locked the door behind me and settled myself on the bed to read the next part of the plan. I couldn't remember what I had read last, it had been a couple of days since I'd looked at it. So, my eyes quickly widened when I saw the chapter I was on now. Chapter thirteen, which had thirteen verses. This was getting ridiculous, what was going on? I read through the chapter and was really taken in by its words and its message. I was in awe of it and what had led up to me reading it in that moment.

It felt like a message for me specifically. Like all of the thirteens that had led up to that moment were like breadcrumbs for me to notice so that I would really take note of that chapter. It was a chapter which focussed on love, and that ultimately love was the most important thing to have. I felt like it was a message from God that he is real and that he loved me, moreover that I should try to live more in love too. Rather than the fear and anxiety that was my status quo. It was a pivotal and special moment in my life looking back; at the time though I was still questioning what was going on. Was I making too much of it and seeing things in all this that weren't there?

The next day I joined the group for breakfast and then followed John out to the circular green at the front where he and others were setting up croquet. Croquet fitted well with the venue we were at, but it didn't seem the obvious activity for us I thought. We were not rich and posh as I would have expected people to be that played croquet. I was intrigued though, and up for having a go at a game that I had never played before. I'd only seen it on television or in films. We played in pairs, which rotated and changed until it was time for lunch. I enjoyed it too.

The group were largely on or around the green or at the swimming pool. The swimming pool was in a large greenhouse type structure and was full of children and parents. I didn't go to the pool because I didn't have a girlfriend, never mind children. I would have struggled with the noise in there too, I could tell that from how loud it sounded from the outside. A large bell started to ring and I realised it was to inform us that lunch was ready.

We filed into the dining room again. I then followed people outside into the nice weather and awkwardly looked for where to sit at the picnic tables. Thankfully I was invited to sit down by a nice couple that I had spoken with a few times at church. I didn't know them that well, but well enough to feel comfortable with accepting the invitation. We ate our food and spoke using the usual social formula. How are you? What do you do? How are you finding it here? Along with other typical lines of conversation. After a while there was just me and the husband sat at the table. We continued our conversation and topics became deeper and veered towards the topic of faith.

I explained the journey that I'd been on so far and the struggles that I'd been having with the Bible and some of the principles of Christianity. I also told him about this strange pattern that was going on where the number thirteen kept showing up in my life and I didn't know what to make of it. I was hoping that he would assure me that I hadn't gone crazy. He chuckled.

"What?"

"You might not believe this, but I live at number 13, which isn't really a common address is it?"

I blew out my cheeks in amazement and a bemused smile formed in my mouth.

As I left for home, I questioned whether I was losing my mind, but I couldn't rationalise how often that number had appeared in my life in quick succession, and at important places and times. Of course, it could be put down to probability and chance, or to my subconscious or even conscious bias. However, I wasn't looking for it when I bought tickets on the day of the Stoke City match. I was just after what was available with a decent view of the game on that day. I also didn't plan to arrive at the assessment centre dead on

13:00 hours, I just wanted to get there in plenty of time, and I didn't choose my candidate number for that day either. They gave it to me. I didn't choose my room number for the church holiday, I was given that when I got there. I also had no idea where the husband I spoke to lived, and certainly not his house number, I barely knew the man.

I believed myself to be a logical and rational man - but I couldn't explain this pattern using logical and rational reasoning. This was something else, something beyond my known world. To my mind, as I drove back out of the grounds down that long driveway the obvious explanation for all of this was God. I couldn't see another answer. I didn't really know what it was for or about, but that seemed to be the most likely explanation to me. It was a way of showing himself to me and that he was with me.

I later received confirmation that I had got through the police assessment centre. I did score low for the task where I nearly gave up and for one or two other areas, but I got 100% for communication which got me through. So, I now needed to wait for the police to perform their vetting process and final checks. Once they were done I would be in.

Then something happened at my current work as a golf lecturer which pushed me over the edge. As a result, I wrote my resignation letter, then sat with it for a couple of days because I didn't know for sure if I had a job to go to or not. Irrespective of that though, I believed it was what I should do according to my own principles. I also believed that it was probable that the police would be offering me a position soon. So, I handed my letter to my boss, and felt a weight lift from me after I did so.

As I was working through my four weeks' notice period my boss informed me that he had been asked for a reference by the police.

"Is that where you're going?" He asked.

"I'm not sure yet, I'm still going through the process." I replied.

That news did give me more confidence that the offer was imminent though. Especially because that request for a reference had happened on the 13th of February 2020. I smiled from the belief that I was moving along the path that God had laid out for me. I had prayed for a new job where I could help people, and as I saw it this news fit the bill.

Chapter 6
History That Changed My World

I left my job as a golf coaching lecturer at the end of February 2020; just before I left I received my job offer from the police. It felt good to leave my struggles there behind me and know that I was due to be moving forward into another career. My start date was at the end of June though. So I needed to decide what I was going to do with the time in between.

I was glad for the time though, I felt it offered me a chance to re-energise before starting with the police. When I resigned from my previous employment, I was prepared mentally to just get another job, whatever that may be, but now I had been offered a career. A future with a decent salary and a decent pension. However, I knew that it was going to be tough and probably dangerous. I was a little apprehensive about the job, but mostly I was excited that I had finally managed to achieve a good career and sorted my future.

Initially I just wanted to take some time off and get away from things. Give my mind and body a chance to recover and heal. I would see my dad more and try to relax and sleep more. I also thought about what I wanted to do while I had the chance because I may be unable to do those things once I started with the police.

One of the things that I decided to do was to be baptised. Our church was due to have a service of baptisms and I asked to be one of the people that would be baptised. A baptism, in the way that it was seen and done at our church at least, was a public declaration of faith. I felt like I was now a believer, God had convinced me of his existence and the messages and lessons of the Bible had become more and more meaningful and real to me as a result. I was willing and happy to declare my faith in God in public, and maybe encourage others in the process.

The other thing I really wanted to do was to go to New Zealand and explore what everybody who had been there said was a really beautiful country. One of my best friends was also living there and so I intended to go and see him too. Before booking my flights though I was waiting for the church to settle on a date for the baptisms. In the end they decided upon April the 12th. Consequently, I booked my outward flight for the 13th and my return flight for the 13th of May. A month would give me a good amount of time to explore New Zealand and create memorable experiences out there. With the baptism and trip booked, I was excited about the interim period to come before starting my new career.

In the meantime, I would spend time with Dad, and do things that I enjoyed, such as go to Parkrun and church. My dad was doing ok at that point. Yes, he was declining as expected with Alzheimer's, but he was doing ok. He had been moved into a new care home, after having to leave the last one. Spaces in suitable care homes were scarce, and we were offered the choice of one about thirty minutes away from where we lived or one about two minutes away. So we chose the one that was closer to us.

The move from the old care home, where he had settled and was relatively happy was a difficult thing to have to do. We had to lie to him about why he was moving. He didn't want to go, which I understood but we had no choice. The home he was currently in informed us that they couldn't provide for his needs anymore, he needed to be in a different home. One that was able to provide more specialised care and cater better for the more complex needs that he now had.

We didn't have long to work out where Dad would go, and it seemed to be the clear choice to go with the one that was close to us. I asked around about the home and was told that it was alright. No real problems to speak of. The reviews on Google weren't good though, but it would be much more difficult to visit him at the other one and he might feel more detached from us. After Dad had moved in I wasn't confident in the new home, which worried me. I wasn't sure about the staff and how they were looking after him. From the beginning he would comment on not liking it and asking to be taken out of there. He claimed that the staff had been shouting at him which was a big concern.

It was difficult to know whether what he said was true or not though. It was hard as it felt like I was betraying him by not taking his word for it. I wasn't listening to my dad though; I was listening to Alzheimer's, that horrible, evil untrustworthy disease. I hated it. I hated the name of it, I hated what it had done to my parents and I hated that it had put me in that situation.

Not really knowing what to do with this information, I hoped that it was because he was now in a place which was not familiar to him and that when he got used to the new place, he would be better. In time he would hopefully be ok. I wasn't sure how I could find out if what he was saying was true. I didn't feel that I could take his word for it, but the staff weren't going to tell me that they had done it either. I considered getting a spy camera and putting it in his room in a teddy bear or something.

It didn't console me that on one occasion we were in the lift going down to go out and one of his carers got in the lift with us. He started to shake even more and looked visibly concerned about her, scared almost, vulnerable. She touched him on the arm and softly told him to calm down, but it didn't ease my concern. It looked more suspicious than comforting, I didn't believe her demeanour was one of compassion. My instinct told me that she hadn't been nice to Dad. I wish I'd said something or done something. It still haunts me now. I just had nothing other than Dad's comments, which I didn't feel were reliable evidence, and my instinct in a lift when the person looked like they were caring for him. I just felt that I had nothing solid to use to say anything or make an accusation.

When I asked him about food, he would tell me that he hadn't eaten. I queried it with the staff, they showed me their written records of his food intake. The records showed that he had been eating and drinking. Multiple times I asked and each time their records contradicted with his claims. This made it even harder to believe his comments about the staff shouting at him and other things. Had he misinterpreted what had happened, was he simply mistaken? Even so, I still regret not saying or doing something about that.

He did settle there more but he never really became comfortable or stopped complaining about the staff. Unfortunately, in time, he also got a bed sore because he wouldn't get out of bed. He would spend nearly all of his day in bed, and as we saw it, the care home hadn't done their part to prevent the sore from happening. They hadn't cleaned him enough or turned him enough or whatever they should have done. So he was sitting on the same area all day and it became infected by who knows what? They had to analyse samples with swabs to work out how to treat it. In the meantime, he was looking ill, his colour was turning paler and he was losing weight.

He was also becoming weaker through not moving and further through the infection. It got to a point where he wasn't able to stand on his own; his legs would shake under the struggle of it. It was a real sign of where he had got to because as a healthy man, he had been blessed with strong legs. Now here he was unable to support his weakened fragile frame. It was a very sad sight which I found upsetting.

It was hard not to feel guilty about what I could have done more or differently to help prevent him getting to that point. It was an impossible situation. Leave him in a care home where I couldn't be sure that they were properly taking care of him. Or take him home and struggle to cope with him myself as a full-time carer. I knew that the practical, emotional and financial toll of doing that would have been too much for me. I just wished I could have faith in the home and trust them to care for him as their title stated.

Despite all of this I still believed that I was ok to go on my trip to New Zealand. The treatment he was and would continue to receive should improve his illness from the infection, and there was little danger to his mortality. He was declining, yes, and had become worse from the bed sore infection but I had no thoughts of him getting close to his end at that stage. So I felt safe to go on the trip. Then everything changed for the worse.

There had been talk of a virus which was spreading across Europe and beyond at the end of 2019. We Brits arrogantly thought it would stay out there though, 'it won't affect us'. Sure enough it arrived on our shores and started to spread across the country. In March 2020 we were all placed under house arrest after the Prime Minister announced on national television that we were to go into lockdown.

This meant that we were unable to see Dad too. Which was hard because he hadn't been in a good state when we had last seen him. I hoped and prayed that he didn't get Covid 19, as it had been named, because I was sure that he wouldn't have the strength to fight it off. He was already trying to fight an infection off with the little strength that he had.

We were not allowed to leave our homes but for short bouts of exercise or necessity only food shopping. It was crazy. I drove out in my car to get food from the shop and the streets were largely deserted. There were hardly any other cars on the road, or people out walking their dogs or riding their bikes. It was like a ghost town out there. I had never seen anything like it. It was surreal, like something out of a film. I felt like I was now living on the Truman Show set, before the actors started to perform their roles.

I was stuck at home. All that there was to do was watch TV, read, write or just find something to occupy myself with. It seemed that many people turned to home improvements and do it yourself projects that they had been meaning to do. That wasn't my inclination, so I watched films and other TV programmes guilt free. I read books and I occupied myself with learning more about things that I was interested in. I was fortunate to be living with my brother, so I still had the social interactions too, even the irritating ones. It must have been a very lonely and sad time in some ways for those that lived on their own.

Airports, of course, were also now in lockdown. There was nobody to check you in, serve you drinks or food, sell you goods or fly the plane. My trip was going to depend on three different countries' approaches to dealing with Covid 19. Dubai was the first destination where I would then connect to another flight travelling to Auckland. It was going to take about twenty-four hours to get from Manchester to Auckland, but that didn't bother me. I had done it before when I was a caddie and flew to the Gold Coast of Australia which was a similar journey. I enjoyed the airports and the flying part actually.

What were Dubai and New Zealand going to do regarding their airports though? Manchester might reopen before the thirteenth of April, but if either of those were locked down then my journey was a nonstarter. This 'trip of a lifetime', which I felt would do me a lot of good and help me to recover and rejuvenate before starting in the police was precarious now. It was looking more likely not to happen, then what would happen to the money that I paid?

It was late March when we went into lockdown, about three weeks before I was due to fly from Manchester. I was resigned to not going, and had become more concerned about my dad than my trip anyway. There were reports of Covid getting into care homes through deliveries that they received, and that people in care homes were dying. 'Please don't let it get into Dad's home'. I thought.

We were able to speak with Dad via video calls. It was great to speak to him, but it was also concerning with how he looked. He was weak and frail, lying in his bed, while one of the carers held her phone in front of him. That was a brilliant thing for her to do as we wouldn't have been able to speak with him otherwise.

Covid 19 was the only real topic of conversation in the media. All of the news coverage was on the rates of infection, the death rates and the immense struggle that the NHS staff were going through to cope. They didn't really understand the disease at that stage. They were informing us while still learning about it themselves. They believed that it was spread from touching where someone else had touched who was infected. They might not know that they were infected though, as many had few or no real symptoms. For some it was a fatal infection or one with an ongoing aftermath called 'Long Covid'. For others it did nothing to them of note or they had what resembled a classic cold.

The government informed the country of the low death rate and how for many it would not result in much of an illness or problem. This served to prevent panic no doubt, which was probably the intention of the government, but it also belittled the costs to some people who suffered greatly from contracting this disease. In many ways it was not taken that seriously as an attitude there developed that it only affected the old people or those that were already ill.

"We should just be able to carry on as normal" people commented. Some people even felt that the government had gone over the top with their lockdown sanctions. 'It's only killing a small minority of us' they moaned, suggesting they should still be allowed to go to the pub or the coffee shop - or whatever else they used to do before this inconvenience. I didn't look favourably upon that attitude with what we were going through. It was selfish and lacked compassion to my mind. It could cost us dearly.

I sat at home worrying that it was going to get into Dad's care home and that he was going to be another person that was just old and already ill. He wasn't just another old person with an illness already though, just part of the 0.02%. He was 50% of my parents and 100% **my dad**. He was **our dad**. He wasn't even that old at 68 either. He also shouldn't have been that ill if the home had done their job properly.

Then in the later stages of April that dreaded call came in. The home informed us that Dad had tested positive for Covid. I felt the horror shoot through my body because to me that news was like being told that he had weeks to live.

He had been an active and fit man for most of his life. Now here we were, in late April 2020, waiting for regular updates about his condition. Was Covid going to be too much for him as expected? We were told that he was getting worse at first, but then after five or six days he was picking up again. That was a big surprise and I started to believe that all of his training and fitness might just pull him through. We were sent a photo of him. He looked flush in his face; his cheeks were red like he might be burning up. Yet still he was grinning for the camera so maybe he was doing ok?

Within a couple of days though, we were informed that he had taken a turn for the worse again. 'Oh no!' Then within the next couple of days the home told us that they were looking into how we might visit him during his final days. All hope was now gone in me. We were offered an opportunity to see him as long as we wore full protective clothing and accepted the risk of catching Covid ourselves. We accepted the invitation and went into the home on a Thursday, covered in plastic and wearing masks. What a sight we must have been for him when we appeared before him.

The first thing we did was tell him who we were. He wasn't very responsive and he looked terrible. He kept coughing up phlegm in his throat and we could hear it gargling as it went back down again, and as he breathed. He could breathe but it wasn't easy for him. We tried to have a more positive and jovial conversation with him, which wasn't easy in such dire circumstances.

I had his brother and sisters on a group video call while we were with him so they could see and speak with him, and he could see or hear them too. These were the last days that they would be able to do that, but they weren't allowed to visit him in person. It was just a horrible situation. Just as we had, his siblings tried to talk to him with a more upbeat and light-hearted manner. Even though their hearts were probably unravelling as they spoke like mine was. In a situation like that you want your last conversations with them to be positive and resemble happy. The sadness could wait, there would be plenty of time for crying and grieving when he's no longer here. In those moments it's about squeezing the final drops of joy and love from your time with them that you can. You owe it to them to try to do that. We owed it to our memory of him.

We went again on the Friday. He certainly wasn't getting better, but he didn't seem to be worse really either. The staff told us that it could be any day though. Again, I called his family and we all spoke with him in a contradictory way to the situation and circumstances we were in. I asked the staff to do something about the phlegm in his throat but apparently the doctors had decided to leave it as the instrument to suck it out may be uncomfortable for him. It wasn't stopping him breathing so they had left it. I wished they had decided to remove it as I stood at the end of his bed, where he could see me.

On the Saturday morning I was feeling it a bit, it was a tough and very sad time. I was about to lose my hero and second parent. My brother said that he was going to visit Dad that morning, but I said that I was going to go in the afternoon. I believed that he would be there still, just a few hours later, to visit, so going for a walk first would be ok. I just wanted some fresh air and to mentally process what was happening.

Not far into my walk I met with one of the pastors from church, Steve, who lived near us. I got speaking with him and we had quite a long conversation. When that was over, and we went to go our separate ways I took my phone out to check for any messages. I saw that I had five missed calls from my brother. Alarm bells started to ring in my head. I instantly rang him back. My brother answered the phone and straight away through his tears he just simply said,

"He's gone".

What! He had tried to call me at the point where it wasn't looking good, but I had been oblivious to it. I hadn't known. Why did I leave my phone on silent or vibrate? Idiot.

I sprinted past Steve, who was walking his dog back home, and ran as fast as I could back to my car. When I arrived in Dad's room at the care home, my brother was stood next to his bed. I broke down crying at the sight of my dad as the reality that he had died hit me, and I hadn't been there. The grief and sadness that I had been holding back came flooding forward and out of me. My brother put his hand on the top of my back to console me, and as a gesture of "Yeh, me too".

It felt like only minutes later we were being asked for the details of the undertakers. I didn't have details to give them, I hadn't thought about it until that moment. So I had to quickly come to my senses and I rang the company that had taken care of Mum's funeral eight years earlier. Mum had died on the 22nd of May 2012. Dad had died on the 2nd of May 2020.

They were both now gone, I just hoped they were now together in heaven.

When Mum died, I walked out of the hospital feeling detached from reality. You could say that I was in a daze. I knew I was walking away from her for the last time, and that I was never going to see her again. I was struggling to get my head around that fact. Never. Never again was I going to see her alive, never going to see her face or talk with her, or at least communicate with her in some way. It wasn't supposed to be this way, it wasn't how nature was supposed to work. It wasn't how life was supposed to work, I was too young and so was she.

I was also aware that this hellish journey towards her ultimate end was now over, and I noticed the weightlessness in my shoulders. I had not felt it before or since. It was the lifting of the weight on my shoulders. They were free from tension and burden, it felt like her final act was to emphasise that I had peace from it now. I did feel a sense of relief that it was over, and that I wasn't having to deal with her decline and everything that went with it anymore.

We pushed open the doors which led back out into the world. The sun had now risen and was beaming down on us from its proud bright, blue sky. The air was still and I felt the warmth of the morning sun on my face. It was at that point that my life continued without her and my brain started to process that she had gone. I turned to my brother and asked him if his shoulders felt the same as mine, and he confirmed that they did. The rising of the sun for a new day signified that life was going on without her, and I must learn to do the same.

I didn't want to comply though, I wasn't ready to, but I knew that I was going to have to. She hadn't just gone on holiday, she wasn't in a home or hospital or just unavailable for a while. She was no longer available to me in any way, shape or form. That was hard to accept. I was only 32 and she had only been 60 years old. It wasn't the natural time for that to happen.

I didn't feel, though, that I really got chance to grieve my mum and process what had happened with her. The battle continued on with my dad, and my gran. In fact, when I dropped Gran back to her house after my mum's funeral, she had an episode while I was talking with her which I feared was a stroke. She just stopped talking mid-sentence and stared into space for what felt like ages, and then said she didn't know what had just happened but her head had felt hot. I phoned for an ambulance. The doctors at the hospital later informed me that it was a reaction to her grief, which had looked like a stroke.

And now eight years after leaving the hospital where I had just watched my mum take her last breath. I walked out of the care home where my dad had taken his last breath but this time I hadn't been there with him when it happened. Again, I walked back out into the world and into the sunshine. I was heavy with the knowledge that I wouldn't be going to visit him again, that I'd seen him for the last time, ever.

I was also concerned about him being near the window which looked onto the main road. I was worried that people would see him lying there in that state, and I knew that he wouldn't want that. There was netting and he wasn't right next to the window so he shouldn't have been visible from the street, but I went round to check anyway. I needed to make sure.

What was I supposed to do next, where should I go? Why were cars still driving by and people still going about their day? My dad had just died, why was the world still carrying on like he was still alive? I just floated around looking for a way to be on my own and process what had happened. I went for a long walk in the woods across the street from where Dad was situated. It was somewhere I could be alone and not be bothered by anyone. The unwinnable battle against Alzheimer's that we had been fighting was over, at least for my parents. I felt vulnerable and exposed. Could I get by ok without them? I wasn't sure. When I fell from this point on, I might just keep falling.

It had taken about 13 years to get to that point, but it had finally happened. They were both gone. I didn't have parents anymore. Nobody there as a safety net, to depend on, to go to with my problems. The guaranteed welcome and support had gone. My comfort zone evaporated. They were where I had always felt safe, away from the world. Knowing that they were on my side, to help and support me. The world was not a nice place, but I always felt safe with them. Even when I wasn't in their company, just knowing that they were there to speak to gave me comfort and a trampoline that when I fell, would help me to bounce back up again.

My focus soon turned to organising the funeral. Choosing the undertakers was sorted. I now needed to sort when and where we were going to do it. The most difficult part though was who was going to be there. We were not allowed to have a service in a church, only an outdoor tribute for about twenty minutes by the graveside. Only ten people could attend which wasn't easy to decide upon. It was up to me and my brother to choose those people. It kind of sorted itself though, with his close family and a few old friends. My brother also set up a group on social media so others could attend in a different way via a live feed, which over 250 people signed up to.

Dad's funeral was on the 19th May and I was due to start with the police on the 29th June. I had about six weeks. The interim period between leaving my job as a golf coaching lecturer and starting with the police had not gone the way I had planned it, to say the least. I hadn't gone on my trip to New Zealand, nor did I feel like I had recuperated. I was actually in a much worse place mentally and emotionally than I had been when I left my employment back in February.

I was now in a daze, trying to mentally process and accept my new situation without him, without parents at all. I thought about Mum a lot. It wasn't just the end of Dad's life for me, it was the end of a journey of over a decade that had led to that point. A journey that had changed me forever, culminating in me looking once more into the same deep hole, where my parents now reside together, under the soil and turf. No longer part of my life, buried with my trampoline.

Chapter 7
Hope of a New Career

At the time of my dad's funeral, I didn't believe that I was going to be ready, emotionally or physically, for starting with the police when the time came, and I was right. I logged into Microsoft Teams from home at 9am on the 29th of June 2020. The rest of my group of student officers were already on there. Due to the pandemic and the government directive to avoid unnecessary human contact we were to do the first ten weeks of our training from home. We had a lot of information thrown at us during that period which I found frustrating and a little demoralising. It was like they were giving us everything as fast as possible so that they could say they had done so later. The daily homework usually took me into the late evening to complete for the following day, as requested.

I wasn't feeling very motivated. I had just lost my dad and was now being subjected to intense training for a job that I wasn't sure that I wanted to do. I also wasn't sure that I was going to be able to do it well, or that it would suit me. I was not a confident person and didn't really like dealing with conflict. If I was confident in a topic, then I would express my opinion, but I typically tried to avoid falling out with people. It bothered me if I thought someone might be upset with me or didn't like me. I knew that was going to be a problem in this job. People insulting and criticising me and challenging what I was doing was going to be a common experience as a policeman. When I was faced with a problem, I tended to ask other people for their thoughts on it. What would they do? What did they think of what I had done or was intending to do? I sought a consensus and reassurance.

I wasn't going to be able to do that in the police really. I was going to need to be assertive and confident, or at least look that way. I knew though, that what was going on in my mind typically showed on my face and in my body language. I've never been able to 'blag it' or 'fake it 'til you make it'. That meant that I was going to need to know my stuff on subjects that I just wasn't that interested in at that time. I was going into a 'good career', but I wasn't confident that it would be a good career for me.

During the early weeks of our training, we attended the headquarters for a day of first aid training and for talks related to the job. Two of which really stuck with me. The first was where the chief constable welcomed us to the service and told us that he now owned us and about 90% of our lives. He would be monitoring our behaviour and would know if we did anything unbefitting of a police officer. That message was not something that I liked or felt encouraged by. I wasn't looking to lose control over my own life; I had had enough of feeling out of control. I was looking to feel more in control if anything.

The other talk was given by a guy from the anti-corruption department, who told us:

"You have never been closer to being in prison than you are now as a police officer."

Oh, good. He assured us that he was on our side and there to protect us, but that was hard to believe. How did, 'You are now close to going to prison' from one of the guys that would investigate that, couple with that person being on my side? I left the headquarters that day feeling like I was at risk, that my decisions and performance were going to be scrutinised closely, and I could easily get into big trouble. I left that day with a firm belief that I needed to avoid making mistakes.

After several weeks my group were allowed to attend classes in person. I was the oldest person in the group by at least ten years. Some of the group were close to twenty years younger than me. I felt like the odd one out and that the rest of the group spoke a different language to me, but then I could often feel that way generally to be fair.

I was given my user name for when I started building my portfolio from practical experience to evidence my ability to do the job. I couldn't help but have a little chuckle to myself when I saw that it was MRidley13. It had become like a crumb that God would leave me to show that I was on the right path and that he was with me. That's how I saw it anyway and it gave me confidence and comfort.

At the end of October, about four months into my training, I received a call from a number beginning with 0113, which I knew was from Leeds - and as I thought, it was the home that my gran was living in. The woman on the other end of the conversation told me that Gran had died. She had gone peacefully in her sleep, which was good to hear. In her early nineties, a combination of Alzheimer's, her old age and Covid 19 had finally moved her on. I thought of Mum, she would have been devastated at this news. It was my responsibility to send Gran off in the way that Mum would have wanted. My first task was to make the arrangements needed to move her body from the home. I had no idea who to call. The staff said they used the funeral home which was close by, and they had always been good. So I phoned them and appointed them to handle my gran's body and arrange the funeral.

Should she be buried or cremated? I didn't know her wishes on that one. Where should she be buried? I had lots of different questions spinning round in my mind, with few answers. I had to inform her family in Canada too and see what her sister might want. In the end we had her cremated like

Grandad, Mum's dad. With regards to the service though, her family and the people that knew her nearby, like her longtime neighbours, weren't able to make it for different reasons.

So, it ended up being just me and my brother with a live stream of the service for her family in Canada to watch. It was a strange experience to remember someone at their funeral service with just the two of us there. I felt sorry for Gran that she was being sent off in that way. We all hope that there will be lots of people at our funeral who will remember us fondly. It added another layer of sadness to the service, that Gran had just us there.

It was also a symbolic end to our journey with Mum, Dad and Gran. Just me and my brother stood in the chapel. I read One Corinthians chapter thirteen out as part of the service. When I got back in the car and turned the engine on, I looked at the clock to see what time it was to estimate what time we would likely arrive home. The clock displayed 1.13pm, which amazed me again, but gave me comfort too.

Weeks later I was at home and gave myself a mental push to order the death certificate. I got the paperwork out that I had been sent by Gran's local council, and looked for the information that would tell me how to order the certificate. I read that I had 84 days from the date of the letter I was reading to order the certificate. I opened the calendar on my phone to work out the date of the deadline. As long as I ordered the certificates before that date then I would be ok.

I counted 84 days forward from the date of the letter and bounced my index finger over the days of the months on the calendar on my phone. When I got to the final days my finger suddenly bounced more slowly, I paused as I realised where my finger was heading.

"Seventy-nine, eighty".

I paused to check if I had got it all wrong. Was I seeing what I thought I was seeing? Then bounced my eyes across the last few dates, "eighty-two, eighty-three,"

until my gaze landed and fixated on the 84th day. It would have been Mum's birthday.

It set my mind in motion, 'Was there any kind of meaning to birthdays or other significant dates?' I wondered. I wrote dates on the notepad in front of me to look at them and think through any possible meaning; focusing on the day, month and last two numbers of the year. I prodded the first one with the nib of my pen, then sat back in amazement. Excitedly I leant forward again and quickly bounced my pen across the second date. I looked at the answer bemused and in wonder then sat back with a wry grin on my face, I couldn't believe it!

There are, I had discovered previously, sixty-six books that make up the Bible, thirty-nine of which were in the Old Testament and twenty-seven that made up the New Testament. My first calculation found that the date of my mum's death added up to thirty-nine, 22 + 5 + 12, and the date of my dad's death, 2 + 5 + 20, added up to twenty-seven. Their deaths, in terms of the dates, represented the Bible, and in the right order too with the Old Testament first and then the New Testament. What were the chances of that being the case? On top of that I'd also realised that my birthday added up to one-one-three. I am literally 113. All of this blew my mind! I was gobsmacked.

Back at work, my first practical experience of policing for real rather than in mock role plays, was when I had a week at a station with one of the leaders of the training department. He had become aware of my struggles because of Irlen Syndrome, so he had decided to help me himself, which was good of him, and I was grateful for it. He fed back to me as the days went by that I was totally capable, but it took me longer than most to do the tasks. I agreed with him. That was what concerned me. Would I be given that time? Would the job allow me to have that time? I doubted it.

I conducted my first interview of a suspect for real that week. It was a low-level incident, but it was big to me. The responsibility of following procedure and asking all the right questions to cover all of the required information was daunting. In our training it had been made clear that a suspect could get away with a crime in court if something hadn't been covered correctly in the interview. The procedure of conducting the interview and the administration that went with it were examples of this. I didn't want to be the cause of the victim not getting the right result. I owed it to them.

Conducting the interview for real was a nerve-racking experience as I wasn't confident in getting the procedure and admin correct, and it needed to be done right. I felt a lot more pressure doing it for real with three other people present than I had done doing the mocks in front of twenty people. The tutor was there to cover that and ensure that things were done as they should be, but I didn't want him to have to step in. That would only highlight my incompetence and inexperience, even though I appeared to be the opposite of that to the suspect because of my age.

"Wow, you really grilled me over that. I've never had an interview that long before", the suspect told me afterwards. I kind of liked that because it meant I had probably covered everything I needed to. But it was also a message of 'that wasn't normal'. That perspective caused me to later question myself, and what I had done, because I had stood out as different to how officers usually work.

The tutor later joked to me and other officers about how much I had grilled the suspect over such a low-level crime. He meant it as encouragement and banter, and I saw the funny side but also thought I obviously took too long and struggled to see why, based on our training and the need to cover all the points. I couldn't understand it.

During that week the tutor asked me about my schedule in terms of placements within the service. I was going to be joining a neighbourhood team first and then was due to go on response. He predicted that neighbourhood policing would suit me better because it had a slower pace, whereas I would hate response as it was a much faster pace and could be relentless. That caused me concern because I was scheduled to be on response for a much longer period of time than for neighbourhood, ten months on response compared with two months on neighbourhood. The opposite of what would have suited me better.

I joined up with the neighbourhood team feeling apprehensive and very aware that I didn't really know what I was doing, which worried me with regards to making mistakes. Consequently, it only made sense to me to let the qualified and more experienced officers that I worked with take the lead on the job. Afterall, they knew what they were doing, and it made more sense to me to watch how they did it for a while first rather than to step in front of them and take the lead. I hated doing things wrong and being criticised for it. I also still had the words from those talks floating around in my mind.

I was encouraged to do the opposite though, to just 'get stuck in' and 'learn from my mistakes.' This created a tension and conflict for me at work because their encouragement to just go and make mistakes and learn from them totally contradicted with what we had been told in my mind. Moreover, my experience of making mistakes in life was that they were embarrassing and confidence sapping because of other peoples' responses to them. Making mistakes or doing things wrong had never made me feel good or encouraged. Making mistakes just brought criticism, insults or mocking from others as far as I knew. I didn't want to experience that on purpose. It was too demoralising, uncomfortable, stressful and demeaning.

This was serious stuff which needed to be done right too. This was the law and peoples' lives that I was dealing with. I couldn't see the sense in knowingly dealing with incidents where I could easily mess it up and then later have to apologise to victims for my ineptitude. That would just be terrible.

Things had gone wrong for me so much in the past that I didn't want to add that kind of guilt and shame to the pile.

I was told by my team leader that student officers should be excited to dive in first and make their arrests and conduct their interviews and investigations. It just made no sense to me though. In no other situation of my life had it been the case that the person that didn't really know what they were doing would take the lead over the person that did know what they were doing. So, there was a friction at large between those two opposing mindsets. I was not being the student officer that I should be, not the type that he said I should be anyway. My version wasn't what they wanted or were hoping for, but their version of training was not what I was hoping for either. The gap between the two was a source of tension and stress.

I struggled to sleep and found the neighbourhood shift pattern tiring. Especially because the first three shifts of the sets were 7am starts and I had a forty-minute drive to the station. I worried about getting up late and about what I would have to do at work the next day. I would lie in bed reflecting on what had happened during the shift I had just been through and how I could have done it better. I struggled to unwind and relax to be able to fall asleep, which caused me extra stress because I knew I had to get up early the next day. I also knew that lack of sleep increased the likelihood of me making mistakes.

When my alarm went off in the morning, I was already awake, it distressed me that the new day had arrived, but I hadn't really slept again. I knew that I wasn't ready for the new day, and just hoped I could survive it. The three early starts really took it out of me and didn't feel like I recovered from them during the rest of the set, as we moved to afternoon starts and late finishes. We also regularly did seven day sets instead of six, for those sets the first four shifts would be 7am starts which was worse still for me.

After a set of shifts I had four days off which were more like three and a half really because the first thing we would do was go to bed after our last shift. I would just feel like I was getting to a more normal energy level again when I would have to set my alarm to start the next set.

Chapter 8
My Exploration of Faith

I was going to church regularly by this point; in fact I couldn't be without it. I had said the prayer which asked Jesus into my life and stated that I will follow him twice. I did it again because I didn't feel that the first time was truly real and authentic. I probably just got caught up in the moment, or felt obliged to go to the front and follow that American pastor. The second time I did it, at my church, I was sure that I was sober in mind and clear on what I was doing and what I believed. I had been going to church for about three years by this stage and so I was much more comfortable with the church and the people in it.

It's a strange thing in a way, faith, because as I see it, there's not really a clear and obvious way to definitively prove it's real to someone else. Like I might do to show that gravity exists by dropping an object to the ground. Indeed, it hadn't been proven to me by another either, through some kind of experiment or demonstration. Yet, by this stage I believed, and still believe, that it had been proven to me. That God had proven himself to be real and true to me. I felt, that it was indisputable based on the evidence that I had experienced, seen, read and heard. That belief had only grown over time.

Early on in my exploration of Christianity I was asking lots of questions to the pastors at the church, who patiently answered them and encouraged me. They gave me books to read on various topics related to Christianity. One of which was on why the Bible could be trusted, and the evidence that had been found which supported and corroborated what the Bible says.

This was a big topic for me because it had been one of my biggest doubts about Christianity, the Bible itself. How could I know that it was what it claimed to be. So, the information I read about how well supported the Bible is by historical evidence and findings really helped me. I discovered that it had an abundance of supporting evidence, far more than any other historical book in fact. Which surprisingly, included from sources outside of Christianity.

I watched a lot of debates on Christianity, Jesus and the existence of God. Including those by a man, who had been a Christian for a long time and was now an atheist. In fact, he was now campaigning against Christianity and hosted a show where people phoned in, and he attempted to show that their beliefs were false and without evidence or substance. He was a big source of my struggle because he spoke to the mindset that I had entered my exploration of Christianity with - wanting to be rational, logical and intellectual. His arguments against Christianity were always ones that I resonated with. I didn't agree with how he spoke to people at times, but I felt that what he said made sense.

The fact that he had been a very intent Christian, who had even considered becoming a pastor but was now a campaigning atheist, also gave his comments more weight. He had very good knowledge of the Bible and could offer his arguments intelligently using information from both sides of the discussion. Which I believed was a good place to be making his arguments from and made them worth listening to.

The value that I placed on his arguments and words dissipated though, when I heard him say words to the effect of;

"I'm not saying that God doesn't exist, I'm saying that there is no evidence which proves that to be true. If that evidence became apparent, then I would say that he exists."

That was the moment that his house of cards collapsed for me, and I detached myself from watching his videos with such interest and regularity.

The evidence for the existence of God as far as I was concerned was indisputable. I could not rationally explain things that had happened to me away. I had read too much which supported the authenticity and credibility of the Bible, and I had come to greatly value the lessons that it offered and depth of its teaching. I had heard too many stories of other people's experiences of healings and other miraculous events. I also just felt so much more at peace through living life in this way. So much so that I would choose to do it whether God existed or not; either way, it was just a better way to live my life.

That will be the sentence that some would say collapses my house of cards, but it was true. Even if I was wrong at the end of all this, I still had the belief that it was the way I wanted to live my life. As time went on, the more convinced I became of God's existence and presence in my life because of the things that happened and evidence that kept convincing me that to be true.

Before I started exploring Christianity, I had done a lot of research on how people work. I also loved to read and watch videos about physics and the way the universe worked. My previous and new research into these scientific areas didn't dissuade me on the subject of God either. There were comments and ideas or findings which challenged me and my beliefs but as time went on they were resolved. I watched world renowned physicists comment on the subject and claim how science proves God doesn't exist and that Christianity or religion generally are not true. One argument they offered - where did the creator of the universe come from, who created the creator, is similar (I think) to how did the universe just explode into existence by a big bang. Where did that original particle come from?

Science has also come to believe that our universe is not based on the certainty of Newtonian physics, but on the probability of quantum mechanics. Well, then, there is room within that universe for God to answer prayer and create events that we describe as miracles. Miracles in that universe are not impossible, just a lot less likely to happen.

There are clear links and repetitions of structure and ways in nature too. Look at the root structure of a tree and that of our lungs. Look at the patterns within the trunk of a tree when it is chopped down and how they compare with our fingerprints. Watch the waves of the sea from the beach and realise that particles move as waves too according to findings from physics, our own brains work through waves even.

The existence of the universe is also so finely balanced mathematically that if it was just to vary ever so slightly one way or the other, from the Gravitational Constant, then it is claimed by physicists that it wouldn't exist. The odds against it existing from that perspective are astronomical and so we are mind bogglingly lucky that it does exist, that we exist. That out of billions of possible numbers the ball landed on the right one, the only one that made life and our existence possible.

Stephen Hawking stated in his book, A Brief History of Time (Bantam Dell Publishing Group, 1988), that the universe seems to be expanding away from us in a way that makes it look like we are at the centre of it. That may just be the case? There are also the lessons and guidance that are contained within and deep under the words of the Bible. For example, I know from my master's degree about how people learn physical skills, that it is typically better for us to focus our attention outside of ourselves, externally. We are also usually more content and fulfilled people when we are focussed away from ourselves too, when we are focussed on helping other people for example. We are better husbands and wives when we focus on our partner's needs rather than our own. We are healthier and more content when we have connections with another person or other people.

What are the two top priorities for us to live by from the Bible? That we should focus away from ourselves on to God and Jesus and that we should love other people and help, care for and treat them with kindness. Living in this way is more likely to fulfil us all too.

We all experience suffering and adversity along the journey of our lives, it is inevitable. All of us will make mistakes and do things that wrong others. Each of us will have wrongs done to us - as we are faulty human beings, surrounded by other faulty human beings. The Bible states that we are fallen people and are living in a fallen world, which certainly has weight to it when I see what goes on in this world. The Bible also states that suffering does us good in some ways because it builds our ability to persevere, it builds our character and builds our hope.

Indeed, this is how we learn and improve our ability to do something, or just grow as people. We learn through suffering and perseverance, and we get stronger and fitter through suffering. After our brains or bodies have suffered, they then adapt and change, hopefully for the better, but that depends on what we are focused on and learn. Nobody becomes physically stronger or fitter through exercises which are really easy to do for them, or more knowledgeable from being taught what they already know. This principle applies generally. To grow and develop, there has to be struggle and suffering involved.

The Bible tells us not to be envious of what other people have and to be grateful for what we do have. Yet we are in a period of time now where mental health and depression seem to be a large-scale problem in our society and world. Much of this has been linked to social media where people are constantly fed a message of how great other people's lives are compared to theirs, from the posts that they see.

We are also bombarded with adverts which try to convince us of how we are missing something from our lives. There is a culture now of always wanting more, more attention, more likes, more followers, more stuff, more money. We are fuelling a self-propagating competition of envy and dissatisfaction. Chasing fulfilment and happiness from what other people say or think of us - and through what we have acquired. Even if that means treading on other people along the way to get better cars, houses, or careers.

There are various theories and mindsets that it is claimed we should adopt these days. We are told that we have the ability to manifest what we want. That we can ask the universe for what we want, and it will provide it for us. There is the law of attraction where we can just think about something we want, and it will come to us. If we are just grateful and think of the things that we want as if they have already happened, that we already own them, then they will be ours one day.

Can I ask, what would happen if every person did these things and got what they wanted? How could every one of us manifest what we want or get it from asking the universe or through the law of attraction? Moreover, would it be a good thing if every person did get what they want? What kind of world would we live in then?

The Bible states that God is in control, that he is good and only wants the best for us, and that he has a plan for this world and each one of us. God promised to provide us with what we need, not what we want. Jesus did say that we should pray like it is already ours, like the law of attraction; the Bible also encouraged us to be grateful for what we have. Grateful to God. Our prayers, though, are not guaranteed to be answered with a 'yes' for what we want and ask for.

We will not receive everything that we pray for, God will say 'no' because it is not in our best interests or because he has a better plan for us. Or it may just be an answer of 'not yet'. We will receive what works for our good, for our growth and development as a person and according to God's plan for the world.

When I was working as a golf lecturer I prayed for a new career where I could help people and use my strengths. When I was employed by the police I believed that my prayer had been answered and that I was meant to help people as a police officer. I wasn't sure that I could do the job that well, but I did believe that God knew better than I did and that he had a plan for me that was for good and to help me to grow as a person and Christian. I discovered during my time in the police that I might be autistic, I'm not sure that would have happened otherwise.

Chapter 9
The Unexpected New Relationship

During the early months of my time in the police John encouraged me to get involved with women again. You know, speak with them, date them etcetera. I wasn't really interested at that point though. I was much more inclined to stay single and save myself from the stress and hassle of dealing with women. Things got too complicated and complex when a woman was involved in my life. I wanted to stay away from any of that as I struggled with my job in the police and with the death of my dad. I was stressed enough from work without adding the complexities of dating a woman on top of that. Life for me was always complex and difficult when it was just me anyway.

I also didn't feel like my time in relationships had gone very well, and that it was probably a lot to do with me. I didn't seem to do or say the right thing at the right time. Women had often become critical of me and frustrated with me. I didn't behave in the way they wanted me to, which made me feel inadequate really - and that I wasn't getting something. The strange thing was that I tended to feel like they weren't getting something too. Either way I didn't like the stress and pressure of needing to become whatever it was that they thought I needed to become. I was probably guilty of thinking the same way towards them too. Noticing and focusing on what would be better for them to do or become. Me and relationships just hadn't been a good mix.

John kept saying it though, and so eventually I succumbed to his nagging. He probably knew better than I did, I thought. I reassured myself that I wasn't going to have to commit to anything just put myself out there again and speak to women. It was exciting in a way, but terrifying at the same time. I often did that, fear how something might go, then get excited and hopeful about it, then find that it went how I feared it would.

I joined a Christian dating app and created a profile. I was nervous about what to put in it and how I would look. I used a photo of me running as my profile picture, a friend had taken it as she supported a local fun run one year and sent it to me. The photo was from the back though as I ran past and away from the camera, so it wasn't your typical profile photo. Especially for a dating app. I thought I'd intrigue women to look at my profile more. If they wanted to see my face, they would need to tap on my profile picture first which would bring up much more of my written information too. I hoped that they would like the sound of who I was, but I wasn't confident.

I had a few conversations with different women which was quite exciting, not that many, but a few. I didn't really know what to say. I was self-conscious because I didn't think I was very interesting or good at small talk and chatting with women. I had learnt that over time. So, the conversations didn't really go anywhere, and I was kind of relieved when they fizzled out because the stress of it was over. I was a little sad about the prospect of always being single too though.

In early October, I was scrolling through the women on the app, when it felt like out of nowhere this woman appeared. It felt that way because it was often the same group of women that I would be scrolling through when I had a look. Which was most days if not daily.

Suddenly this classy looking lady called Clare was there, and I was taken by her instantly. She had a short blonde bob hair cut which was down to about her jaw line, with large (steady fellas) dark framed glasses, and big (easy lads) lips with red lipstick on. She was wearing a tight white top which went up to her neck but had a more see-through pattern across her chest which made it sexy too.

She was the woman that I'd been most attracted to, so much so in fact that I quickly resigned myself to not having a chance with her. She wouldn't be interested in me I thought, I haven't got the right credentials or verbal patter. She looked sophisticated and self-assured which I was not. I was about to swipe her across and move on to the next woman when a voice in my mind said;

"Stuff it, what is there to lose? You never know."

So I messaged her, without any real expectation of a reply.

I carried on with my day and tried to focus on other things. I went to work, ate, drank, slept and talked rubbish with my brother at home as normal. In the back of my mind, or maybe even the side or front, I was wondering what she would do. Will she reply? Nah, but what if she did, what would I do then? The pressure would be on me to impress her like one of those wildlife programmes where the male bird does a strange dance and shows off his feathers.

When I went on the app again the next day, I was surprised to find that she had replied to me. Not only that, but she also seemed to be enthusiastic too. It was disconcerting, that wasn't how it was meant to go. Her response was very upbeat and almost excited about speaking with me. The guy who she could only see the back of his head. I wasn't sure what to make of it.

It wasn't long before she was suggesting that we scrap the app and communicate through our phones instead. The problem with that was that the app wouldn't let you write numbers in the messages, but Clare found a clever way around it. So, I messaged her phone for the first time like

I was conducting a sound check, and she replied excitedly. Then we were off!

Messages were pinging back and forth as we chatted like we had known each other for years, not days. It became clear quickly that Clare was funny, there might have been a screw loose somewhere, but she was great to speak to and I always felt more uplifted after our conversations. She was so positive and upbeat, looking to find the humour or positive in everything.

I have a dry sense of humour based on one-line comments, which Clare laughed at and regularly offered her own which I found funny too. The conversations were very easy and flowed well for hours at a time. It suited me that they were via written messages as I was able to process what she said and then consider what to say back. We got on that well, we soon progressed to the idea of meeting up. I felt a pressure to come up with something and somewhere that would be interesting and impressive or cool, the type of suggestion that women would be after. I didn't feel though, like I was that guy, who knew that kind of information for where to go or what to do for a date.

I'd heard people talk of going for a coffee or for a drink at first. In many ways the pressure on me was lifted by the situation we were all in. Social distancing was in play and a lot of places were closed, so the only way that we could meet was to be outdoors. That way the chance of us passing Covid 19 was significantly reduced apparently, according to the government instructions and guidance. So we agreed to meet for a walk.

I had never been to or even heard of the place where we were meeting, so I followed the sat-nav and parked up in the designated car park. I couldn't see Clare anywhere, so I got out of my car and went to the parking meter. When I turned around with my ticket, she was stood right in front of me, about 30 yards away. She was looking to her left and right as I walked towards her. She looked at me finally, but then looked to her right and left again.

'She has no idea what I look like' I thought, which surprised me. There were photos of my face in my profile, but she couldn't have seen them. She'd turned up to meet me - a stranger, that she wouldn't know if I bumped into her. 'I'm going to need to help her out here', I decided.

"Hi Clare."

I called from about ten yards away. She turned her head forwards towards me, and then with a big smile said

"Oh, hello, you must be Martin."

I couldn't resist asking if she had known what I looked like, and she confirmed that she didn't but she liked talking with me and how I came across. She had said in our conversations that she didn't care about looks but I thought she would want to know what I look like at least to be able to identify me.

We set off on our walk and the conversation set off at the same time. After about ten yards she stopped and asked me to repeat what I'd just said. The date could have been over already. I repeated what I'd said and with relief she started walking again as she realised that she'd misheard me. She laughed it off as we carried on. She was good fun and easy to talk to. I didn't feel intimidated or too nervous, despite the mishap at the start.

A further surprise was when Clare told me that she had children because I'd set my profile up on the dating app to connect with women that didn't have children. I had had two experiences of going out with single parents and I hadn't enjoyed that dynamic in either case. Maybe I just wasn't the right person for that role? I hadn't liked being the add on to a family, it was a very difficult position to be in. It was a powerless position where I didn't have the authority a dad would have, which made dealing with behaviour issues difficult. It was also made clear to me by the children at times, that I wasn't wanted or welcome in their family which did hurt to some degree.

I found it to be a miserable situation for me to be in, which was why I was looking for a woman that didn't have kids. I knew though, that this would reduce the number of women around my age that would be in that position. They were likely to be few. When Clare said she had two kids I was confused about why we had been connected. Or was it that she'd told the app that she didn't have kids? She assured me that wasn't the case, and she was as confused as me. They were more like adults though really. Her son was 19 and her daughter was 15 at the time.

The government had banned us from mixing with people outside of our household so Clare's son had moved in with his girlfriend's family so they could see each other. I took solace in that it wasn't the same as it had been with previous relationships where the children had been primary school age. I enjoyed her company and was grateful back at the car park when she gave me a chilli she had made. Surprised, but grateful.

Clare and I continued to go for walks, and continued to chat via messages and video calls. The video calls made me nervous and stressed, with having to do small talk live and maintain an interesting conversation. I was out of my comfort zone. Clare was just happy to talk with me though, it was like it was enough for her that I was in front of her and there to talk to. To be honest she wasn't short of words, so I didn't have to come up with that much conversation, listening was my main task which I was good at. When the conversation did dry up for a moment, she would just look at me and smile. That was good but also confusing for me because nothing had happened, I hadn't said or done anything. She seemed to be just smiling to smile. I smiled back, I think, awkwardly.

As a topic for me to talk about, I told her my story around the number thirteen. I knew that it was probably not the best story to tell her, after all I sounded like a nut job. I knew that, but I told her anyway. She told me later that she did think it was weird and it caused her to wonder about me at the time. Just after we ended that call though, I received a message from Clare.

"I feel a bit funny in my tummy. I get off the phone from you and my friend sends me a photo. Completely unaware of our conversation. She said she was drawn to it so now looking up the meaning of it in the bible. Are you ready for it...."

Clare then sent me a screen shot of the photo. It was a photo of the number thirteen which was on a house or something similar, which her friend had seen while out during the day.

"I'm shaking", Clare continued. *"Why did she feel the need to send it to me at that moment?? Wow...xx"*

I replied with laughing emoji's and

"It's definitely all in my mind"

"Crazy!"

Her friend was a keen photographer and said that she'd been drawn to taking the photo but didn't know why. It was an incredible thing to happen and helped to solidify my beliefs further on what had happened for me. It also changed Clare's thoughts on my story too.

The government later introduced a concept and rule which involved us being in 'social bubbles'. That would mean that we could have contact with one other household apart from our own. I went into a bubble with Clare. We hadn't been seeing each other long so it wasn't a straight-forward decision because it would mean not being able to see other people in our lives who we'd known for longer. If we didn't though, then we wouldn't be able to see each other at all for who knows how long. Which might have made it increasingly difficult to keep our relationship going.

So from that point on I spent my time with my brother at home, at work or at Clare's. She would make us dinner and we would watch films or just chat with music on in the background. We continued to get on well and she continued to make me laugh which was something I really liked about her. She was always so happy to see me and so joyful it was infectious. I found it slightly strange for her to be that way towards me, why would someone be that happy to see me, there must be a catch somewhere? The more I saw her though, the more I got used to it and accepted it. To be honest I wished I was more like her.

I tended to go round Clare's in my rest days, as they're called in the police. She lived in Stafford which was 13 miles from where I lived, had done for 13 years by that stage she said, and her house was closest to junction 13 of the motorway. Facts that got my attention as you can imagine. I was able to go round a little more during my first rotation because the police station was closer to where she lived. When I was on response though, closer to my home, the shift pattern just didn't make it reasonable to drive to hers and back after work. So I would typically go round during my rest days, but rest was what I needed because I was exhausted.

The church services had now moved online because we weren't able to congregate in person. I missed it, I felt like I was able to re-energise to some extent when I was at church. Singing with a group of people in praise of God, listening to the lessons from God's words and sharing that space of faith with other people rejuvenated me. The online versions were still good, but not the same. I would even have to miss the online services at times due to work and catch up at a later time. Clare and I would sit together and watch them though, which was good to do.

I needed that weekly rejuvenation too because I was really struggling at work as part of the response shift, just as predicted. I found myself turning up for shifts already shattered before I started. The shift pattern was difficult for me to adapt to and cope with, as was the work and demands that were placed upon me as a response officer. I struggled through at first when I had a tutor with me, and we would work through the jobs together. Although she often did a larger portion of the paperwork than me to get it done quicker and enable us to go home sooner.

I was struggling to get my head round all the different things that we had to do, and the different ways that we needed to do them depending upon what we were dealing with. There were so many forms to fill in, some of them duplicates of what we had already done. It seemed to me that people further down the line wanted us to save them time, so we had to write the same information two or three times. I wasn't sure what I was doing and was working too slowly, so my tutor tended to take the slack and accept that I would do what I could and that she would do the rest.

While I was grateful to her for doing that, I also felt quite useless and worried about how I would get on when I was on my own later down the line. I needed to learn this stuff, but I was too shattered to take it in while we were trying to get it done as fast as possible. I understood why that was the case because after a nine hour shift you just wanted to go home, especially when it was after midnight or seven in the morning after a night shift.

However, with regards to my learning and development it was not ideal. I also felt like a burden for my tutor because she was having to work such long hours with me as her responsibility. I knew that to a large extent it was the nature of the job and just how it went, but I also knew that it was because of me too. It seemed like nearly every shift we were working an hour or two over which obviously shortened the gap between ending one shift and starting the next. Therefore, it felt more intense and that I didn't really have much of a break from work in between shifts.

I would leave work later than I was meant to, feeling exhausted, and arrived home with little energy. I managed to cook myself something to eat, but did little else. I went to bed hoping, praying, that I would be able to get some sleep to give me a chance for the next day. I tried everything I could to be able to sleep, but while my eyes were closed my brain was still revving and my body was tense and tight from the day or days that I'd had. After a while I couldn't help but look at what time it was, and would see that I now had six hours available for sleep. Later, I would look again and see that I had four and a half hours. Until my body would have the horror shoot through it as my ears registered that my alarm was going off for the next day, or next shift. Oh, no.

The set of shifts would come to an end after a second night shift in a row. I was desperate for sleep and rest for as long as possible, but when the sun was out, and neighbours were making noise it was difficult to do. I would often wake up just a few hours later in the late morning or early afternoon and then struggle to get to sleep again. So, I would get out of bed and hope that I was able to sleep that night instead, which would typically be at Clare's.

I would stay over at Clare's quite often during my rest days, partly because of the distance between our houses, but mostly so we could see each other longer. I really liked being in her company and spending time with her. I'd never met anybody like her, she lived in a world that was very different to the one that I was living in. She would celebrate the simplest of things and make the most trivial and mundane of things seem fun and funny. I just loved being with her.

The difficulty for me though, was that I struggled to sleep at her house too. In fact, I probably slept slightly worse because of being in a different bed and having someone lying next to me. I couldn't have things just as I wanted them which played on my mind. I tended to lie very still when trying to sleep, whereas Clare would move much more than me and I would be distracted by it. I liked being away from home and away from the stresses and problems that our home caused me, but I didn't like not being able to sleep when I was so desperate for it. I was conscious of the need for me to try to catch up on my sleep before the next set of shifts. That never happened as well as I would have hoped though, wherever I slept. So it was better to be with Clare and away from home.

Chapter 10
'November Delta Four Six to YF...'

At the start of my career in the police I was trained intensely for about three months on the rules of operation and the laws of the country that we were to serve. I would be working in a small part of that country, but ultimately that was what I was to do. After all we had sworn allegiance to serve the Queen to the best of our ability and with humility and sacrifice. We'd been told that we were being watched closely and were accountable for our actions, both in and out of work. The rules of service for us as officers were clear. The law that we were to apply was set out in writing too.

I found though, that the theory of how to be a police officer was different to actually being a police officer. The things that we'd been told in training didn't seem to be followed fully in reality. The ways that had been clearly taught to us didn't seem to be how the officers I was working among seemed to do the job. They cut some of the corners due to the limited number of officers and resources that they were working with. They didn't have time to do it by the book. That caused me confusion and anxiety as I was conscious of performing the role as they had trained us to do.

I worried that we might get in to trouble by not sticking strictly to the rules and how we were trained to perform the job. After all, we'd never been closer to being in prison, and were being watched continuously. At any moment some faceless person could question me on something I'd done, or not done, and I would have to account for my actions. I also knew that, 'I was following what my colleagues told me to do', wasn't going to get me off the hook. I was only accountable for my actions from my own decisions - that had been made abundantly clear. I was my own person as far as they were concerned, separate from the influence of others.

That greatly troubled me. I didn't want to upset my colleagues. I didn't want to upset my tutors, but I also didn't want to get in trouble with the anti-corruption department or my superiors. I was told on numerous occasions not to worry about making mistakes, but it didn't really help. I always worried about making mistakes, and now the consequences of doing so could be so severe and dire. How could I not worry? It seemed that everyone was conscious of it at least; there was a clear culture of everyone making sure they covered their own backside, which then contradicted with the expressed ethos of family, unity and togetherness.

I was typically feeling unsure, foggy, and tired. The fear of getting things wrong clouded my mind and I constantly questioned my own knowledge and decisions. This fear of making mistakes actually caused them at times, I'm sure. They weren't big mistakes really, but they were to me and negatively affected my confidence and assurance of my ability to do the job.

There were times when I even made a complete mess of saying the caution when I arrested people. I said the early part of it wrongly and then tried to rescue it but got more and more into a mess and made a complete hash of it.

"You are under arrest. You do not have to say anything. But if this goes to court and you are asked questions then it could be a problem for you. In that case anything you say could be used as your story, but if you don't tell us anything now then they may not listen to your version of events and think you're lying."

My tutor looked at me bemused. "What was that?"

I didn't know either, and started again. I got it right in practice no problem, but when doing it for real my brain became scrambled on occasions, and I would have to do it again correctly.

"You don't need to say anything. But, it may harm your defence if you do not mention when questioned something which you later rely on in court. Anything you do say may be given in evidence."

Simple, how could I mess it up?

The other student officers in my group seemed to be loving the job and flying through the different tasks that we had to evidence in our portfolios. Successfully conducted an interview of a suspect, tick. Safely searched a person, tick. Spoken correctly on the radio, "November delta four six to YF….", tick and so on.

I was behind and it was agreed that I was to be supervised by my tutor for longer than planned while we tried to complete phase one of my practical training. I wasn't surprised that it was taking me longer than the others, but it still affected my confidence as I felt sub-standard compared with the other student officers in my cohort and generally. I felt like a problem. That said, I also welcomed the continued support from my tutor who I had gelled well with.

There was a clear highlight during this period too though. Me and my tutor were sent to an address to help with a missing person incident. As we made our way there in the police car at speed with the blue lights flashing, an adrenaline inducing event in itself, my tutor asked me what we needed to do when we got to the address. After I had given her my answer, she told me that I was going to lead on the enquiry when we got there. She said that she was confident I could do it. That surprised me but also felt good to have her vote of confidence. I continued to rehearse what I'd need to do in my mind. There were certain things that I would need to do and ask which would then be relayed to other officers looking for the missing person, or 'miss-per' as they're called in the police. It was very important that I did them all correctly and efficiently for the well-being of the miss-per, and for the best use of police resources in trying to find them.

One of our guidelines was to stay at the address and let other officers conduct the search. We were switched over to a specialised channel where only officers dealing with this missing person were listening in and communicating. There was a big concern for the person as they had made worrying remarks when they left the house, and they were drunk. It was also late at night and very cold, down towards zero or below, so cold that my nose was running and I could see my breath under the street lights. I had under layers on, woolly gloves and a hat as well as my stab vest which made me warm usually, plus a fleece jacket and bright yellow overcoat. Still, I felt the cold.

I completed all the tasks that I needed to do, including searching the address and asking all the questions about the person's appearance, name, circumstances and where they might go. There was nothing more to do other than wait, wait in case they came home, or there was something else to find out from the family. We chatted politely with the partner and offered them reassurance as they kindly made us a cup of tea. It helped to keep them calmer too by doing something normal.

As I listened to the radio through my ear piece though, it was clear that the search was taking place at least a mile away from the home.

"I want to go do a search round here." I said to my tutor, asking for her permission.

"We need to stay at the house."

Which was a good answer, following the procedure she knew from her training. 'He could be just down the road where nobody is looking though', I thought.

I became more and more restless, more convinced that I needed to go look in the area close to the home. My body wasn't moving but I could feel it getting twitchy, like it was saying 'come on, we need to go!' The noise in my mind and body built and built until I couldn't take it anymore. About twenty minutes after asking her, I started walking towards the front door.

"I'm going to go look round here."

"Ok, don't go too far."

That was all she said, which surprised me as I'd been ready for her resistance. Maybe she realised how adamant I was?

I walked back out into the freezing cold night and followed my breath. There was a field nearby which was empty, then I made my way down the street towards the canal. It was pitch black down there. As I crossed over the bridge above the canal, I decided to go to the right first. All I could see was what my torch showed me in its cone of light. It was eerily quiet in the darkness, and I was very aware of being alone. After about sixty yards I turned around and went back to the other side of the bridge and continued in the opposite direction.

There was a mist over the water and nothing but the canal on my left, trees on my right and the pathway in front of me. There was room among the trees and so I thought the person could be in amongst them at some point, so my eyes and ears were on alert. I walked forward, alone in the silence and darkness. The only noise was from my footsteps and the sound of my breath, with the occasional rustling of the leaves.

It was like I was walking towards a black tunnel as I moved further and further away from the home and the street lights. I was conscious that I was meant to be in the house and that I could get in trouble for that, but I knew I should continue.

Although, that belief was starting to fade, and I was beginning to think that I had misinterpreted my gut feeling. 'I'll turn back', I thought. 'No, I'll go to where that grassy bank is up there where there's room behind it. Then I'll go back.' A deal was struck.

I arrived next to where the grassy bank was, about four to five feet in height and a perfect cover from the elements and people I thought. I couldn't see anything of note for finding the miss-per and could just hear the leaves rustling. Then the rustling died down and my ears locked onto a sound that didn't belong, it wasn't one that I'd heard so far and not one that I recognised from nature. I quickly made my way up the grass mound as the soil gave way under my feet. I got to the top and the noise was louder still, I shone my torch downwards among the trees and spotted a person lying on the ground fully clothed. I cautiously made my way over to them and saw that it was our missing person, I recognised him from the photos I'd seen at the house.

WHOOSH! The excitement and adrenaline rushed through my body, I quickly celebrated my find with a quick clenching of my fist and a smile on my face. Just before I found the person, I'd heard the control room talking with the police helicopter pilots to come and help with the search. I knew that would cost thousands of pounds. I had to let them know as soon as possible. It was definitely our miss-per!

"November delta four six to YF".

"Go ahead four six".

"I'VE FOUND THEM". I said excitedly.

"Ok four six, have you checked for ID to confirm it's them?"

"Oh", I said, dejected.

"Erm I didn't realise I could do that, it's definitely them though".

My tutor suddenly came on the air asking where I was, I could tell that she was running as she spoke.

"Down on the canal, go down to the bridge and turn left, I'm about two hundred yards along".

Suddenly I heard thick, solid boot soles banging on concrete from above the bridge in the distance,

"MARTIN", my tutor shouted.

"YF, I'm nearby I'll go to assist too". Another officer informed control.

"I'M HERE". I shouted back to my tutor.

I knew that the person would be ok as they were on their side and were clearly breathing ok as they slept, so I went onto the path and waited using my torch as a sign for the other officers.

There was a pause as I waited in the silence and occasional rustling of the leaves, then I saw light appear on the corner of the path in the distance and it got gradually brighter and bigger. The two officers then appeared and came running round the corner to me. I showed them to the person's location, and then while they picked the person up I found their ID.

"November delta four six to YF". I said with gusto.

"Go ahead four six".

"Just to confirm that I have now checked their ID and it is definitely them, can you get us an ambulance please". I said proudly, while also thinking 'I told you it was them'.

"Thank you four six. All patrols, all patrols, you can stop your search, repeat the person has been found. Thank you for your efforts".

We took their weight as they were struggling to walk and helped them all the way back up onto the bridge over the canal, where the ambulance met with us and the paramedics took over. We helped them get the person into the ambulance while my tutor went back to the home to let the partner know the good news. The missing person sat in the ambulance with a blanket around their shoulders. They were slowly coming round.

"How did you find me?" They asked, bemused.

My tutor was back by this point.

"That was down to my colleague here, he found you. It's a good job he did, you could have died spending the night out in this cold. He could have saved your life".

I felt the grin form on my face and the warmth build in my body despite the cold.

The miss-per looked at me again with a confused and bewildered expression on their face.

"How did you find me?" They repeated, like they thought it was impossible.

"I don't know, I just followed my gut."

The missing person shook their head in amazement, then settled themselves on the bed and lay down.

'I could have saved their life', I thought. It was a very proud and meaningful moment, one of the best of my life. If I did nothing else right in the police, then that was worth being in the job for by itself.

Chapter 11
That Explains Things

I was keen to help the public and treat people appropriately and proportionately, with compassion as much as I could. I was keen to not break the rules and not get into trouble too. I was also keen to fit in with my colleagues and feel like I belonged with the shift I was working in. That was what they called the group that you worked with regularly, the shift.

It became clear to me that the response shift officers I was working with had a bond between them and a certain sense of pride in being part of that shift. I didn't want to be perceived as someone that went against their code or way of working, I hoped and wanted to be seen as part of their shift. I also though, wanted to be comfortable with my actions if I was questioned, and according to my own conscience.

As response officers we had to attend the incidents, make arrests, take them to custody, complete the initial paperwork, conduct the follow up investigations and paperwork, then send it off to the Crown Prosecution Service (CPS). Typically, the whole process needed to be completed and resolved within six months. The CPS though, could respond with a list of tasks that they wanted doing before they would process the case and make a decision on whether it would be taken forward to court or not. Which did happen to me once and left me with about twelve tasks to do.

Six months might sound like a long time but that included the CPS process too, so really we had three or four months to do this because the CPS were backed up with demand themselves. Add to that, that we were in work for six days out of every ten, so four out of ten wouldn't be used. We were also, nearly always short staffed, and each shift some of us would be tasked with watching cameras at custody, sitting with prisoners at hospital, investigating missing persons or helping the mental health practitioner. It was like a football team trying to compete with nine men. A good portion of us were student officers learning the job too.

Each shift there was a list of the incidents that we needed to deal with as a group, and we had to keep the number as low as we could. They were graded as either grade one or grade two predominantly. A grade one incident was an emergency where we needed to get there as soon as possible. Grade two incidents weren't emergencies but still needed dealing with as soon as we could, when we weren't dealing with grade ones. The grade one incidents seemed to come in straight away, where some of us wouldn't even be able to stay for the briefing at the start of the shift. They came in constantly from then on usually too. They would quieten down during a night shift though.

After I eventually completed the first stage of my portfolio, I became responsible for my own investigations. My pile gradually got bigger and bigger as the sets went by. I could feel the weight of them increase as time went on. I felt like I was gradually sinking more and more and was unable to stop it. I was advised to be more proactive and assertive in completing my part of these investigations, but I found that very difficult to do.

I had to investigate incidents that I had attended during previous days or weeks when there were gaps between incidents for the current day. Those gaps were typically small and few and far between. There were two big problems with this for me, as I saw it. The first was that I was always in the passenger seat and never the driver of a car, so it was difficult to just decide to go somewhere for my investigations. Secondly, our shift pattern meant that there were even more limitations on when I could do it. Two of the shifts were night shifts so they were a write off, there wasn't much I could do between 10pm and 7am. I also found it difficult to do paperwork in the quieter times of a night shift because I was so tired. My body was fully aware that I was awake when I should have been asleep.

After discounting the night shifts, we actually had a rolling sequence of four days out of every ten, to complete investigations. There was very little time or chance to do this during those shifts, which put a lot of emphasis on doing it quickly and taking any slight opportunity. I found this difficult to do with the authority of a student officer. For example, I was often given the tasks of watching cameras at custody or sitting in hospitals with offenders for hours. Moreover, the qualified officers that I worked with had their own stuff to do, which obviously took priority for them.

There was also the writing room, as they called it, or the office as it is normally known. It was not an environment that suited me at all. It was a large open planned room in the shape of a capital L. Across the bottom of the L there were rows of desks and computers where the inspectors and sergeants would sit. Up the length of the L there was about eight rows of desks and computers with stations on either side of the rows for officers to use. The ceiling was white with large tiles, and with several of those tile spaces filled with bright white lights.

I was often alerted to people leaving or coming into the room from either end, as I heard the door hinges moving and the doors opening or closing. There was a distinctive noise when they opened and then when they shut again. I could hear keyboards being struck as fingers tap danced across the keys, and the distinctive sound of the space bar in between the letters of the words.

There were the voices of people talking about incidents or other topics, the volume going up and down as they made each other laugh or stressed their points. Officers calling other officers across the room, almost forcing me to look up for the other officer and see what was so urgent that they couldn't walk twenty yards to talk to them.

There was the control room constantly talking into my ear piece, which I needed to listen to in case they said mine or my partner's call sign. Sending us to a grade one perhaps, or to hear the alarm of a code red because a colleague was in urgent need of help. There was constant communication on there between the control room and officers.

The false light of the computer screen strained my eyes and alarmed my brain; it also drained my energy. The bright white light above my head shone down on me like a spotlight at the theatre, and reflected back up into my face from the shiny desk and computer that I was working from. I could feel the headache coming on and the fatigue gradually increasing as the frame rate of my cognitions and movements gradually decreased. The longer I sat there the slower I became both mentally and physically.

I needed to be in a darker and calmer space which was quieter for my senses. I needed to be able to relax rather than be on alert, without the pressure of doing the work as fast as possible while knowing that I might need to stop doing it at any second. There were occasions where they tried to give me some time to do my work, but then had to send me out to something such as watch cameras or attend an incident. I was all they had left. Time and time again this happened, meaning I didn't make much headway.

I was exhausted. The combination of my struggle to sleep, the shift pattern, and struggle to meet the demands of the job got on top of me. I was stressed, very stressed. I started to notice a knot in the centre of my chest, it was like a tightness under the top of my sternum. It seemed to just appear, I wasn't sure when it started, but it wasn't going away. I had conversations with one of the sergeants and admitted how much I was struggling.

I carried on for weeks with that knot in my chest and the feeling of being highly stressed and exhausted. I was drowning and didn't feel like I had the strength to stop it. All the strength I had was just slowing down the rate at which I was sinking into the quicksand. I couldn't see a way out of the mess that I was in. I started to question my future as a police officer and question my own abilities to be a normal member of society. I kept turning up and kept going, even though it was literally harming me to do so.

Why couldn't I do this job like all the other officers? They didn't seem to be more intelligent than me, but they were clearly different to me. What was it about me that was making this so difficult and affecting my health so badly? I thought about my dad and how impressed he'd been that I was joining the police when I told him in his room at the care home. Even though he wasn't here anymore I felt like I was letting him down again, just like I had as a young footballer.

I was conscious that I'd previously sworn never to put my job above my health – yet once again I found myself in that predicament; my health suffering, with the cause seemingly linked to my job, my new career. The knot in my chest was only getting worse, my stress levels were only getting worse, my exhaustion was certainly not getting better. Then I noticed that there were small circular patches in my hair, where there was no hair. It looked like my hair was falling out. That was too much, the final straw. I booked an appointment with my doctor.

I was signed off work to help me recover, which I didn't like, but did feel it was necessary to try and recover and recoup. To allow my mind to settle down and my body to relax again. That didn't seem to really happen though. The thought of going back to work triggered the very things that I was hoping would subside so that I could go back and do myself justice. I was in a strange place mentally because I believed that I was an intelligent person - not in all ways, but in ways that should be able to do the job well. I believed I had the personal skills too. However, I didn't have confidence in myself to do the job how they wanted me to do it, or at the pace that they required of me. I waited for my body and mind to calm down, but it wasn't really happening, and I wasn't sure what to do about it.

I was in a good career; it was solving a lot of my financial concerns regarding the present and the future. It was a good job. I probably wouldn't get another opportunity like that again. Without that job I was probably going to struggle badly for work and an income. I had to make it work somehow but I couldn't see how.

The knot in my chest was still there, my body was tense, my mind was foggy and I could feel the emotions sprinting through my body. I wasn't sure what to do with myself at home, now living alone in my own house. The guilt of being at home weighed on me too. The shift was one more person less with me off, even though I didn't think I would be a big miss. Society had made it clear that not working was what lazy good for nothing people did too. Was that what I had become now? I felt like it.

I received a call from occupational health, the woman that rang me informed me that she had been looking into Irlen Syndrome, which I had put on my application. She said that her research had informed her that people with Irlen Syndrome often have other difficulties or conditions too. She said that I could go for a neurodiversity assessment if I wanted to, which they would organise. I agreed.

I went to the assessment, which was conducted by a clinical psychologist, and completed the various tests. At the end of the two or three hour session he was to inform me of his findings. I was nervous but excited while trying not to show it. What was he going to say? What if he says that I'm completely normal and there was nothing different about me from the norm? Then I'm just not good enough for work and for all sorts of things in life. If, however, he says that he has found something then I'm not just rubbish, then I have an explanation for being different, and why I struggle when I shouldn't be struggling.

My answers had been honest and without prejudice, I was comfortable that he was assessing me on my situation. In fact, if anything, I had been too cautious in my answers not to say something was the case when it wasn't. Later, when I drove home I realised that I had done that too well, and would have scored even higher than I did had I not been so mindful of that.

The clinical psychologist informed me that the results suggested that I had clinical traits of autism. Wow. I was 41 years old. Mum had always said that she thought Dad was autistic, and I thought I might be too. I was relieved and a slight grin formed in my mouth. I had walked into the building feeling the weight of the world on my shoulders. I had been looking for some kind of explanation for my struggles with the police, and over the 41 years of my life to date. I walked back out of the building with the explanation I was hoping for, I was autistic, or at least it looked that way.

It just made so much sense to me, it felt right. I drove home with my mind playing numerous different movies of my past. All those moments where people were criticising or shouting at my autism. My struggles in the workplace which could be explained by being autistic. I was excited by this revelation and explanation for why I wasn't just weird and rubbish.

I later thought about my dad too. A lot of the stuff that I had been angry and upset about could be explained by him being autistic also. After receiving a form of diagnosis for me I felt quite sure that he had been autistic, but we hadn't known. So much of his behaviour and ways could be explained by this new perspective and framing. I wished we had known this while he was alive, I wished I had seen him that way while he was alive. Rather than seeing him as strange and frustrating, infuriating even.

I felt my anger towards him crumble, and forgiveness took its place. He hadn't behaved the way he had to upset me, ignore my wishes or make my life harder. He was just ill with Alzheimer's and was probably autistic himself. His criticisms of my character as a young footballer was his way of trying to help me be better and as good as I could be. When he talked of beer calming him down and that he needed it, he was also talking about the calm it brought to his senses and their over stimulated state. I realised that I experienced the same feeling when I drank beer too. This would also explain why he struggled with small talk and with change, such as my Mum's illness and its affects. He was likely autistic, and I had inherited it from him. I felt bad about how I had behaved towards him through my ignorance.

I wished he had talked about what was going through his head more. He didn't do it at all. Before Mum's illness I had tried in various ways to get him to do it and help him but he couldn't bring himself to talk with me about how he felt and what he thought. I don't think he wanted to show any signs of weakness. Something that I came across with several men while I was in the police. They were in a desperate state to a large extent because they hadn't spoken to anyone about how they felt; instead they drank alcohol to escape it and just carried on. I had realised that Dad's approach was not the one that I should take in the future. To not talk and just carry on only caused more destruction, more weakness and more despair.

When I had spoken with my sergeant, I explained my difficulties with trying to work in the writing room and all of the sensory distractions and stimulation which I found overwhelming. I told him that there was software I could have, and had used before, which made it easier for me. Therefore, a request went to HR for me to have a laptop computer so that it could have that software on it, and I could go do the work in a better environment for me. That request went on and on and was chased for six months or more by one of my inspectors, but never materialised. In my early days as an officer another officer had told me that people with disabilities like us had to fight to get help and adjustments from the service. This proved his point.

I had four to six line managers in ten months while I was on the response shift. It was like they were each taking the hit for a while and then it was only fair that somebody else took a turn. That's not what they told me of course. It was because the new line manager really wanted to help me, or because they were overwhelmed with people they had to manage. It did little for my confidence to be passed around like an unwanted pet though.

I was included in an email chain over a period of time between HR and other relevant parties, such as a sergeant and inspector on my shift. The final email of that conversation came through shortly before I returned to work. It said that they couldn't change the lighting in every writing room and police station, or the set-up of almost every device just for me, and that the police should have considered this more before they employed me.

That email broke me and after I read it my body felt like it was in free fall. I hadn't asked for the lighting in every police station to be changed just for me, I just said there was software that helps me, and finding somewhere quieter and darker than the writing room would help too. Which was why a laptop with the software on it could have really helped me. I read that email as them saying that I wasn't being reasonable, or that it wasn't reasonable for them to try to help me, and that they shouldn't have employed me in the first place. So where did that leave me?

I went back to work trying to forget that email. I tried to go back hopeful that my situation could be resolved and that I could qualify and have a career in the police. At first, I was back with the response shift for a short while before I was due to have a break and then rotate to a different department at custody. I didn't pick up investigations because I was due to move on, so I was ok on lighter duties as they eased me back in.

The first day of the new rotation though, I hadn't really slept the night before and I felt like my body had nothing to really give. It was like my body wasn't willing to work for them anymore. A feeling that I recognised. I turned up for the next day feeling even worse, and I ended up going home because I wasn't in a fit state to work. I thought I just needed sleep, I felt desperate for sleep. I was back where I'd come from to a large extent.

What was I to do? This couldn't go on. I prayed to God for help and for a solution to this awful situation I found myself in. I had managed to be employed in a good career again, just like football when I was younger and as a golf lecturer, but it was a nightmare for me again, just like they had been. I reflected and reflected on the situation and how it could be resolved, what could I do differently? I hoped for a clear message from God of what to do.

Randomly, my mind focussed on the street that the police station was situated on where I'd worked for several months. It had always struck me as a strange name and maybe one from history? I looked it up on Google maps and was reminded that it was called Bethesda Street. That could even be from the Bible I thought, and so I Googled it.

It was from the Bible. I discovered that it was from the book of John, chapter five and this is what I read.

'The Healing at the Pool

Sometime later, Jesus went up to Jerusalem for one of the Jewish festivals. Now there is in Jerusalem near the Sheep Gate a pool, which in Aramaic is called Bethesda and which is surrounded by five covered colonnades. Here a great number of disabled people used to lie – the blind, the lame, the paralyzed. One who was there had been an invalid for thirty-eight years. When Jesus saw him lying there and learned that he had been in this condition for a long time, he asked him, "Do you want to get well?"

"Sir," the invalid replied, "I have no one to help me into the pool when the water is stirred. While I am trying to get in, someone else goes down ahead of me."

Then Jesus said to him, "Get up! Pick up your mat and walk." At once the man was cured; he picked up his mat and walked.'

And so, I felt the message was clear that I should leave the police, as scary as it was. Jesus instructed the man to walk in verse eight, it gave it more weight for me still that chapter five plus verse eight was thirteen. So, I notified them of my required four week notice and left the police with no idea what I would do next. I was gutted that it hadn't worked out and felt like a failure again. I questioned whether I could have a professional life like everybody else. I did understand myself like never before though, and felt that I should use that knowledge to work out what path to take moving forward.

Through my research into autism and autistic people I had come to understand that they usually have a couple of things that they are really good at and really interested in. Upon reflection, I quickly concluded that mine were coaching and writing. So, I decided that I would focus on those two areas for what to do next, and shortly after leaving the police, I started writing this book.

Chapter 12
A New Life Begins

My scheduled baptism hadn't taken place in 2020 due to the covid pandemic and the social distancing regulations. So the following year when we were allowed to do it again I asked to be baptised when an opportunity arose. Clare went to church with me that day and supported me from the audience as I explained to the church why I was being baptised. The date was the twenty-third of May 2021. This was what I read out to the church, looking at Clare now and again for reassurance.

"Why am I here, being baptised today?
That is the question I am to answer.
Well, I'm here because of what's been,
And is yet to come,
I'm here because the time is right,
And this is the place,
I'm here standing on the shoulders of Jesus,
Who met with me and gradually raised me to my feet,
And saved me from my despair and hopelessness.

I'm here today as a failed footballer,
That for so long grieved over that lost identity,
Yet God drew me towards him and said, "you are mine".
I'm here today after years of mourning who I am,
With other peoples' words still corrupting my mind,

Yet God tells me he loves me as I am,
It's my heart that matters to him.
I'm here today after years of hoping to achieve people's approval,
Yet God says I designed you this way,
And Jesus says come as you are.

I'm here today because my mum was cruelly taken from me,
Because I watched my biggest fan slowly drift away over five years.
Yet Jesus tells me he loves me even more than she did,
Which is hard to comprehend.
I'm here because last year my hero was taken from me too,
My dad also taken by the same cruel disease as my mum.
Yet Jesus chose to die for me, and for them.

I'm here today because four years ago
I went down on my knees,
And prayed to the God that I didn't believe in,
Desperately asking for help because I had had enough.
I'm here today because a few months after that day I was invited to Parkrun,
Which brought me into this church for coffee afterwards,
And introduced me to more people from the church.
I'm here today because that gave me the impetus to explore God more,
To challenge it and study Christianity,
To wrestle with it and what people would think of me.
I'm here today because instead of wrestling with it I was advised to live it,
So I started a conversation with God,
And the peace I felt as a result was deafening.
It was exhilarating to finally find such peace,
And I have gradually got lighter since as my iron suit fell to the ground.
I'm here today because of the many signs I believe I've had from God,
That said, "I'm with you."

That showed me I'm walking his path,
And living out his plan for me.

May is a tough month for me,
It is the month that both my parents passed away in,
My dad last year at the beginning of May,
And my mum, nine years ago yesterday.
So, I'm here today because it perfectly represents my rebirth,
My new start and new life.
It is the day that will remind me of my hope, faith and love,
That will lift me up each year after remembering my parents,
And the life I used to be.
I will focus on who I am this day,
A child of God,
A follower of Jesus.
And while my parents rest in peace,
I now know that Jesus is the way to peace in life.

I'm here today because of this Church.
Because of Steve, James and Henry,
Because of their help and patience.
I'm here today because of its members,
Because of their help and encouragement,
Because of their Bible study groups and small groups.

I'm here today because of all my failings,
Because of all of my suffering,
And the lessons learned.
I'm here today because of lots of events and circumstances,
Big and small,
And through the influence of everyone I've ever met.
I'm here today because of the help of many people,
And the lessons learned.
I'm here today because of the good in my heart,
And the good I want to be.
I'm here because the Lord lit the runway in my darkness,

> And led me to his light.
>
> Why am I here today being baptised?
> Ultimately, the answer to that question belongs to God,
> It was his plan,
> And being here today was irresistible for me."

About one month later Clare and I took the opportunity to go away for a week in late June 2021. We chose to go to Keswick in the Lake District. For those that have been to the Lake District you'll know that it's an area to go for long walks and hikes up mountains. Of course, Clare arrived there with just thin ankle socks. I tried my best to warn her about walking or climbing with those socks on.

"It'll be fine Mart."

She did at least have walking boots on, but I was sure of what was going to happen, blisters.

The first walk we did was to go around Lake Derwentwater, which was near to Keswick town centre, as we made our way to Cats Bells. A row of hills which were on the far side of the lake. I thought I'd start Clare off with a smaller climb first before we tried a proper mountain. We had a coffee first of course; it was a bright warm sunny day so as we sat outside the coffee shop chatting and watching the world go by, it made perfect sense. It was lovely and I could certainly feel the warmth of the sun.

Clare loved coffee, almost to the point of obsession, no almost about it actually. It was something that really struck me about her when I started going round her house, how much coffee she drank.

"Cuppa tea?"

She would ask in her Essex accent and warm, smiley tone, before bringing me a cup of coffee, which puzzled me. She was like a chain drinker. I would be drinking that 'cuppa tea' when she would ask over her shoulder,

"Cuppa tea?"

I would look at her as she walked towards the kitchen with a confused expression on my face and then politely decline. I was still drinking the first one. Once again she came back from the kitchen with a coffee and I realised that she wasn't actually asking me if I wanted a cup of tea.

To get to Cat Bells we also had to walk around a part of the town to begin with. As we walked I could feel the top of my head getting hot and I was conscious that my cap was in the car rather than protecting my head. I stopped in my tracks. Clare stopped too and looked round at me with a curious expression.

"What's up?"

"I've got to go back to the car."

"What, why?" She asked again, somewhat alarmed.

"I need my cap. I'm going to get burnt on my head without it."

"But we've come so far Mart."

I laughed out loud.

"What?"

"Clare, we've literally just started for how far we have to walk yet, it's going to take three or four hours, and if I'm going to get it, I need to do it now because we're walking away from the car."

Clare laughed too.

"Oh, ok, I'll wait here then".

We both eventually made it up to the top of Cat Bells, from where we had an amazing view of Keswick and the surrounding lakes and rolling hills.

Two days later we attempted to climb Helvellyn, or Helsinki as she called it. About half-way up the mountain Clare was struggling; her blisters were really hurting her, and her legs were getting sore. She said that she couldn't go on and that she would meet me back at the car. As it was, I couldn't go much further either because I got to a point where I couldn't see much more than the path or rocks in front of me due to a thick fog. It looked like one wrong move and I could fall into the fog either side of the route forward. 'Stuff that', I thought, and I caught her up as we made our way back down the mountain. She was really struggling, but still she smiled and made jokes, laughing as she went.

That was just typical of her to make even a painful scenario for her a fun experience for me, and her in a way. As we got towards the bottom and close to the car park there was a set of stairs that had been created in the hill and stoney pathway. It was too painful for her to go down the steps forwards, so when I looked back from the bottom, she was effectively tacking down the stairs like a sailboat travelling into the wind. Walking diagonally across the stairs one at a time, like she was walking across hot coals.

I started laughing as I watched her make her way down the stairs. She noticed and then morphed into pointing the index finger on each hand and moved with a dancing walk which could have had the song *Staying Alive* playing in the background. It was hilarious, and I laughed raucously as I watched her perform her entry to the school of silly walks all the way to the bottom, laughing herself as she went.

"You might have been right about the socks Mart", Clare conceded.

From then on, we spent more time doing light activities because of her struggles, Clare with her new socks on. We mostly just spent time chatting in nice settings, and thoroughly enjoyed it too. I loved being with her, she made me smile and laugh a lot. There were so many highlights within the week just because of how she was and saw the world, and how we bounced off each other.

During our stay we had seen that there was a crazy golf course in Hope Park, close to the lake. I was a keen golfer that had qualified as a professional coach, and Clare kept saying that we should have a game before we go home. So, on the last day she said that she would take me on, even though she hadn't played before. The first hole went as expected with me managing a comfortable score of two and Clare getting four. Fair enough.

From then on though, things did not go as expected at all. Clare wasn't holding her putter right, she wasn't standing or aiming right, and she didn't particularly strike the ball that well. On the second hole though, she got a hole in one, and we celebrated and laughed over her unexpected success. We then moved onto the third hole where Clare got a hole in one again, and we looked at each other in disbelief, celebrated and laughed. As we played the holes Clare was starting to make comments about her prowess at golf and how good she was at it. She put her ball down again to start a hole, miss-hit the ball, sending it in the wrong direction than even she was intending to send it. The ball hit rocks and obstacles, popped up in the air and bounced off things multiple times.

"No way, you're kidding me." I muttered.

Her ball slowly made its way around a bend on a slope then crept up to the hole before dropping to the bottom.

That was her sixth hole in one. I looked over to her, gobsmacked, as she dropped her putter onto the grass nearby, and walked off with her palms held up in front of her shoulders, waving her hands from side to side in disbelief. The comedy of it was hurting her body as she laughed at her latest ace. She put her hand over her mouth as she tried to compose herself again, circling back to where her putter lay. I was laughing uncontrollably too, mostly at her reaction and comments. She came back with her putter in hand.

"I can't play on Mart, it's going to kill me if I carry on, I'm literally going to die of laughing."

Overall, she had eight holes in ones out of eighteen holes, a number of them defied logic and caused us both to question our grip on reality as we sat down for a coffee after the round with smiles on our faces. Thankfully I had just managed to beat her score overall and maintain my dignity.

The next morning with our bellies like stuffed laundry bags from the cooked breakfast, which was epic, we set off back home. I was driving; as we left the village we were staying in, and I pulled out on to the main road out of Keswick I realised that I had a big grin in my face. Nothing had happened or been said to cause that grin in that moment. I was just happy. For no real reason, it just struck me. I couldn't remember going away for a holiday and leaving for home with that grin or that feeling of happiness before. That knowledge of what a great time I'd had with another person. It was captivating.

The memory of that grin and that feeling as we left for home stayed with me. I was still working in the police at that point, and as I continued through my struggles as a student officer my mind would sometimes go back to that moment. I would reflect on how much I had enjoyed being with Clare that week and how happy I had felt at the end of it. I wondered if she would be interested in marriage, in marrying me. I couldn't remember feeling that happy before, it was certainly unfamiliar to me. I wanted to get to know it better. To be attached to it permanently.

She continued to make me laugh and smile and feel valued. I'd not received her kind of welcome from anybody else, except for one person. She was always so happy to see me even though I wasn't sure I deserved or warranted her apparent delight at receiving my company. She said hello with so much enthusiasm, wearing a smile which consumed my gaze with her immaculate teeth shining back at me. I wondered if she'd had her teeth done, they were so healthy and perfect looking. It was typically followed by a hug and her favourite question.

"Cuppa tea?"

I found our relationship difficult in some ways, as I had with all of my previous relationships. There were complexities that I wrestled with repeatedly as I traversed the days and weeks. As always, my mind was consumed by the various conundrums as I looked at the corners of my world. I often felt like I was being pulled by all of them at the same time but knew that I couldn't go in multiple directions at once. Without my parents, I was very conscious of the fact that I was fending for myself and that my decisions had to be right and productive for my current and future well-being. I was always conscious of my well-being. I could feel my blood travelling round my veins at times, or the fatigue in my bones. I was conscious of the weight of my brow and eye lids too. Was it right or fair to put another person through my struggles with me? Could I handle adding their difficulties and stresses to mine?

During the summer of 2021, Steve the pastor, told me that he was going to plant a new church locally and asked me if I would be interested in joining him. If you're not familiar with the term of 'planting' this is the process of branching off from another church to encourage new people to attend, but in a different area. I had some hesitation because our current church had become familiar for me, but I recognised that I didn't really feel part of that church and it would be better to try a new one. So, I agreed to follow him, and liked the idea of being part of a smaller church and a closer-knit group. It was a slight risk but one worth taking I felt.

Before the church launched, I asked Steve to put Clare into the church messaging group too. Clare had been going to one near to where she lived, but she agreed to start going with me to Steve's new church despite the journey for her. It was a big step in a way, and an act of commitment by both of us, but an important one for our relationship. The name of the new church was a fitting one, Hope Church.

There was about thirty of us that turned up for the first service of the new church. We were located in St. John's Church community hall, which made me think of my dad because the new venue had his name in it. The service was recorded, and the video was uploaded onto the internet for people to watch. I found it later that evening and was stunned again to see that the video of the first service at 'Hope' was 113 minutes long. It caused me to think of One Corinthians chapter thirteen again, and gave me encouragement that I was where God wanted me to be.

Clare and I both loved it at our new church from the very start. There was a real family feel to it and a connected spirit between us all that helped to found it. It was exciting to be part of this new start-up and work together to help it grow, which it did. The rest of the church took to Clare quickly too, her warm, cheery demeanour and sense of humour made her popular from the beginning. She soon became a face that many of the others looked forward to seeing.

Christmas was soon nearly upon us. I found myself checking the time on my phone early one morning. It was about 6am, and I also noticed that I'd received a message. When I looked to see what it was, I realised it was from Clare. She was going to hospital after experiencing cramps and bleeding. She had been experiencing pains in her stomach for days before this and I had urged her to see a doctor.

"It'll be alright. I need to go to work", she said.

It had now come to a head, clearly.

After seeing her message, I quickly got out of bed, put some clothes on and got ready to leave the house.

"I'm on my way." I messaged her.

When I got to her house, she didn't sing her usual welcome or offer me a drink. She was solemn and clearly upset. As soon as I entered the house, she pulled me into the living room and closed the door behind us because her daughter was upstairs.

She said that she'd phoned the NHS helpline and the woman told her that it sounded like she'd had a miscarriage. I was shocked. 'We were pregnant?' I thought. A tsunami of thoughts flooded my mind before I quickly snapped myself out of that daze again and focused on Clare.

"Ok, I'll take you to the hospital, have you got what you need?"

"Really?"

"Yes, of course. Have you got everything you need?"

"Err, yes, I think so, oh…"

Clare went to get something else, and say goodbye to her daughter.

When we got to the hospital I went into the A&E reception with her. It was very quiet and sparse of people in there which was a strange sight I thought for an A&E. We walked to the counter, it had a big glass partition between us and the woman on the other side. In front of the other members of the public waiting to be called through, Clare then had to explain why we were there. It annoyed me that she had to do that in front of those strangers with such an upsetting situation, such a mentally vulnerable one for her. That kind of thing should be discussed in much more privacy for me. She was telling my private information too which I wasn't comfortable with but what could we do?

The woman then informed us that Clare would need to wait before she would be called through. Ok, we'll have to join the others in the waiting area. She then also said that I wasn't allowed to stay with Clare due to covid restrictions. What?! My heart sank as that information landed in my ears like a cannon ball landing on a concrete floor. I tried to persuade the woman to let me stay given the circumstances, but she wasn't allowed to let that happen. I looked at Clare feeling heartbroken for her, the fact that she was going to have to go in there alone. Have a miscarriage alone, and who knows what she would have to go through in the process.

I felt like I was letting her down. I should be with her as she goes through this. I didn't know what to say other than sorry that I can't stay. Clare assured me that it was ok and that she would be ok, but we both knew that she didn't really mean it. We hugged tightly.

"I love you." Clare said through her tears.

"I love you too."

Then I kissed her goodbye and left. I felt terrible and almost emasculated as I walked back out of the building, leaving Clare and her wet face alone with strangers to deal with whatever was going to come her way. Unable to protect her.

As I walked to the car my mind started to relax again and let thoughts in, thoughts which were from my perspective. What was going to happen in there? I could have been a dad? How would we have coped? Have we lost our child today? Will we lose our child? I didn't know what to do with myself, so I drove home again, and as the thoughts continued to race around in my mind they built up to a crescendo, and I burst into tears.

All I could do at home was wait to hear from Clare. I decided to go to the golf club and play with the lads as planned, at least I would be occupied rather than just sitting in the agony of waiting for news. I joined them for breakfast as was customary, and about twenty minutes later Clare phoned me.

"Hello."

She said with some light back in her voice. They had told her that she was still pregnant and was probably fine but needed further tests and checks. Clare joked and laughed about the situation which was typical of her. What a relief, but at the same time we still didn't know if our baby was ok or not.

We went for the follow up appointment. I was allowed to stay with her this time which was good news. I was with her as they performed a scan to look for any sign of a baby, but no signs were there. I looked at the screen intently, it was a jumble of black and grey shapes, but I couldn't see anything that resembled our baby.

"It might be because it's so early." The doctor said.

"It might be there, but we can't see it yet."

There was a grain of hope, but it didn't look good. It was now going to be about monitoring Clare's hCG numbers, which should go up if she was pregnant.

As we left the hospital Clare was not hopeful at all, but for some reason I was. I found myself believing in God and his power more than ever before. He could make this happen and give us a child, make this pregnancy healthy and successful. It occurred to me how strong my faith in God really was in that moment. I was adamant that God could make it right, that he was in control. I prayed and prayed and insisted on staying hopeful and faithful. I didn't mean to question Clare's faith here, that's just where I found myself. The truth is - I was a little surprised by how strong my own faith was at that point in time.

We were scheduled to go back a few days later to see what her hCG numbers were. They had gone up when she was tested alongside having the scan, which was encouraging. However, when we went back her numbers had fallen again. That was a bad sign, and one that confirmed Clare's feelings for her. When we went back again just before Christmas, her numbers had fallen again. The reality of it was starting to sink in and my hope was evaporating.

We were going to lose the pregnancy. We were going to lose our child. It was now just a matter of time. There was no need any more to ponder how we would decorate the second bedroom, or what name we might give to a boy or a girl. Those things wouldn't be needed.

Returning home and then turning our attention to the time of year, the question that then faced us was 'what should we do for Christmas Day?' We certainly weren't in the festive mood. Was it even right for us to do Christmas Day as normal? Almost pretending that everything was fine when it wasn't. I knew that we were going to be miserable, or certainly not jolly, but I said that we would have a Christmas Day at my house. I would cook the dinner and we would just watch films or something and spend the day together alone.

So, I put a load of pineapple up a dead duck's derriere and cooked us a Christmas dinner, which we ate together in the conservatory with the heater on. Nice it was too. We drank some wine and tried to make the best of it. We chuckled at our feeble jokes and made polite conversation through the meal, before sitting on the sofa in front of the telly. We got through it. As we sat on the sofa after dinner Clare turned to me.

"Did you think it was a boy or a girl?"

"I felt like it was a boy."

"Yeah, I did too." She smiled.

"What name were you thinking for a boy? Hang on, we'll both say our names at the same time."

"Ready?"

"Yep." I replied.

"Three, two, one."

"John."

"John."

We both spoke together and laughed. I thought of my dad for a few seconds, and then looked at the drawing of my mum hanging on the wall. The drawing I had spent days doing after she died as a way of staying connected to her. I would have loved to have had a son and name him after my dad and keep his memory alive in that way. To keep our family line going too. I would have loved for both of them to be still here with me and tell them that they were going to be grandparents. Mum would have been ecstatic with that big beaming smile of hers, and Dad would have shaken my hand with that proud look on his face which said, "Well done son." I'd seen that face on occasion.

The following day, Boxing Day, I was sat downstairs having breakfast when Clare came out of the bathroom upstairs and called down to me.

"Mart, it's definitely happening."

A jolt of horror shot through my body, before I got up from the sofa and put my dish and cup in the kitchen. I knew what it meant, but Clare didn't need me to instantly arrive in front of her at that moment. I could hear the distress in her voice and felt that she needed calmness from me. I also needed a moment to process the reality that I knew we were in and what lay before us before I acted. I knew it was going to be horrendous.

We went straight to the hospital. We'd been told what to look out for and where to go if and when it happened, so we arrived at the reception we were instructed to go to. Again, there was a glass partition between us and the woman on the other side, but we didn't have an audience this time, thankfully. I explained to her that Clare was having a miscarriage. She took some information from us and informed me that I wouldn't be able to stay.

"I'm sorry but there is no way that I'm leaving Clare here to have a miscarriage on her own." I replied with intensity.

"I'm sorry, but it's the rules we have to operate by at the moment." She stated.

"I understand that, but I am not leaving here to let Clare go through this alone; that's the rule that I'm operating by."

Her face dropped down slightly as she looked up at me from her chair, she took a breath and her expression changed to one where I could see her sympathy and empathy for what we were going through.

"I'll go see what I can do."

"Thank you." I said in appreciation.

We were shown to the waiting room where we sat alone for hours. I sat there with tears in my eyes and a ball of sadness lodged in my throat, with my arm around Clare as she cried on my shoulder. When she was finally seen I went in with her. They examined her but the doctors and nurses wouldn't answer my questions directly about our situation and what was happening. They were probably concerned about saying something that got them into trouble. After they left, I went out of the room and looked for somebody more senior to gain some clarity and got some answers. I returned to Clare knowing for sure that we were having a miscarriage.

Clare was examined again, and eventually we were faced with our pregnancy held up for us to see in a little plastic container. It was horrific for us both, but particularly Clare. They asked us what we wanted to do with it and how we wanted to say goodbye. I couldn't answer the question as I looked at the small pot, nor could Clare. I wasn't prepared for the question or for what I was looking at when it was asked. What to do with whatever was in that small pot which should have become our baby? It was absurd that something so small should represent the extreme pain and emotions that we were experiencing.

We were taken back into the waiting room. As we sat there alone again, traumatised, I held Clare as she rested her head on my shoulder. I could feel the rhythm of her pain as she sobbed. After a while when the waves of her sadness had calmed down to ripples, I said;

"We need to pray, Clare."

"Ok."

She slowly lifted her head from my shoulder. I then prayed to God to help us get through this.

I walked Clare back to the car with my arm around her. Again, I was in one of those moments, like I had been with my parents, where I had to go back to doing normal things when it didn't seem appropriate. To just drive ourselves home again. Clare was in that space with me too this time. The grief and sadness got into the car with us, drove home with us and walked through the front door with us. It was in the tea that we drank and the idea of having something to eat that we pondered. It all seemed wrong!

Why had this happened? Was God punishing us? Was it our fault? Why did I have to lose a baby on top of my parents? Why this too? Who did I need to be for Clare now? What did she need from me? What should I do for my own grief and mental health? Again, lots of questions but not many answers.

We went back to Clare's house so that she could be back in the comfort of her own home. I stayed with her and stopped overnight. The next morning, as the light invaded the room from around the curtains. I was already awake as Clare woke up.

"Oh Mart, for a moment there I forgot that it had happened."

"I know, that was a nice moment you had there, it's ok, I know how you feel."

I cuddled her as I tried to offer some comfort. I was all too familiar with the grief we were going through.

We moved into that period of nothingness that passes between Boxing Day and New Year. We did nothing other than spend the time together. The days went by with Clare's face often on my shoulder. There was nothing I could say or do to ease this pain for her. All I could do was put my arms around her. I couldn't answer her questions. I couldn't offer her reasons. I could only be with her.

As we moved into the final days of December my mind reminded me of that time in my car, with Clare in the passenger seat. It reminded me of that unprovoked grin that I could feel in my mouth and face as we pulled out onto the main road out of Keswick. I remembered being on my landing at home, weeks after that trip, with that same grin on my face again. Then laughing to myself, I recalled all the things that had happened or things that Clare had said.

I reflected on how often I had found myself sat in my car waiting for the traffic lights to turn green, laughing at something Clare had said or done or simply smiling over our time together. So often I would think of her, and a smile would pull at my face. How she greeted me when I arrived at her house, always so happy to see me. The conversations and laughs that we would have, the laughs often leaping out from behind the topics we were talking about and taking me by surprise. She was the only person I needed. She was the only person that had ever made me that happy, even when I'm not even with her.

She was the person that I wanted to have a 'cuppa tea' with for the rest of my life. I knew that each one would be different and probably enjoyable. I loved the sunshine that filled a room when she was in it. I loved how she made me laugh and smile, and the way she made me feel. I loved how she loved me. I loved how I loved her. I struggled to love who I was, but I loved who we were. We were like two halves of a lock which fitted together securely and filled the gaps of the other half. It was better being me when I was with her.

I prayed to God for his guidance. I mulled it over to make sure it was right, but I knew it was. This was as big as it gets, so I had to make sure it was what I wanted and was right for both of us. That it wasn't a reaction or response to what had just happened. My mind wandered back to hoovering my landing, to waiting at traffic lights or driving my car to work laughing or smiling because of Clare. I pictured her gorgeous face and radiant smile, as we sat with our coffees or ate our dinners. The dinners often created the comedy themselves as she created something new. This was what I wanted and what I should do. I was sure of it.

So, on New Year's Eve we were at my golf club and sat at our table, with my mum's ring in the inside pocket of my coat. I was ruminating about when the right time would be, as I spoke with Clare. There were three other couples sat at the same table as us. The old couple next to me turned out to be Christians too and the husband mentioned to us that he carried a guardian angel in his pocket. I instantly thought of our child and asked if I could see it. He pulled a cotton hanker chief out of his inside jacket pocket and gently placed it on the table in front of me, then carefully unfolded it.

Inside the handkerchief was a small faceless angel about three centimetres tall and lying on its back. It looked like it had been sculpted out of a large pearl, with silver wings. As I sat there looking at that tiny angel, I thought of our baby John. I could feel the emotion and wonder in my body as I held that angel in my fingers. It was all I could look at as I thought about him. It gave me a sense of comfort that he was ok, and God was looking after him. Hopefully he was with my parents. Baby John with Grandad John. I would meet John one day; in the meantime, my parents would look after him.

After we had finished our meal and the disco had begun, my mind turned to the task I had left to do. We both had a drink, which I thought we might need, like we were just going to tap glasses and say cheers afterwards. So I said to Clare;

"I'm just going to the toilet, but when I get back, I'm going to tell you a story."

The perfect set-up, just like the movies. I knew the story was going to take a while, and I needed to go.

"Err, oh, ok."

She replied laughing, not knowing what to make of it.

I went to the toilet and as I washed my hands, I looked at myself in the mirror, said nothing, just looked into my own eyes. I was sure, and I was ready. So, I walked back out and sat down again next to Clare. I could feel the nerves in my veins. Telling stories was not something I thought I was good at, therefore it wasn't something I did very often; I wasn't sure how it was going to go. I took a drink of my beer, then turned to Clare,

"Are you ready to hear my story?"

"Yes Mart."

I adjusted myself on my seat and rested my arms on the table with my hands together and fingers interwoven.

"Well, in 2017 I found myself on my knees in my bedroom praying to a God that I didn't believe in, asking him for help because I couldn't take anymore, due to the death of my mum and illness of my dad and Gran."

Clare's face was a little bemused by the start of my story, it didn't exactly sound like one that befitted celebrating the arrival of a new year. Not exactly a story of hope.

"Ah Mart."

She said with sympathy. I continued.

"Shortly after that I was invited to Parkrun and God led me to the church next to the park, and a sense of peace that I had not known before came over me when I started to pray to him. Then the number 13 repeatedly appeared in my life, and the next reading on the plan I was going through was 1 Corinthians, chapter 13. Which was all about love. The thirteenth verse says, 'And now these three remain; faith, hope and love, but the greatest of these is love'."

"About four or five months after my dad's death I reluctantly set up a profile on a Christian dating site. It just so happened that just after I did that, a gorgeous blonde lady did the same. When I saw her, I thought I had no chance with her, but then she replied to my message, and I couldn't believe it. As soon as we started talking it was like we couldn't stop. We shouldn't have even been matched by the site, but we were."

Clare was leaning in a little more by this stage. I continued.

"I was in a dark place after losing my dad and struggling with life generally, but this woman brought sunshine into my life and often caused a smile on my face. We're just such a great fit and she's such an amazing person, as she often reminds me."

Clare laughed.

"And I know that I want to be with her for the rest of my life. In fact, when we left Keswick in early July, I knew it. I even did a Google search after we got back of the local jewellers and took my Mum's engagement ring in to be resized for her. I've had it ready at home ever since. The address of the jeweller that I took it to because it had the best rating turned out to be 113 High Street, which made me think of One Corinthians thirteen and God's hand in it."

Clare blew out her cheeks and smiled.

"I was planning on doing it at Christmas, but then a heartbreaking thing happened, and I wasn't sure that I could or should do it anymore in those sad circumstances. But I also knew that what had happened didn't change how I felt about her or about wanting to spend my life with her."

"And so",

I reached into my coat pocket for the box. Clare spotted what I had pulled out and her eyes widened. I continued.

"It just remains for me to say."

I moved my chair out of the way and went down onto one knee, then opened the box to show her my mum's engagement ring.

"Clare, will you marry me?"

Her eyes were full of tears by now as she tried to see the ring.

"Yes."

She replied, just about squeezing the word out of her throat. I put the ring on her finger, and she threw her arms around my neck. We held onto each other tightly for several seconds.

When we released ourselves from the squeeze, I looked around us, but it was clear that nobody else on our table realised what had just happened. So Clare announced it to them and made sure they knew. We had been seen earlier by people I knew from another table and so when I turned around, they were all looking over at us with big smiles on their faces. They had noticed what had just happened. They raised their hands into the air in celebration with a cheer. Shortly afterwards, the bar manager brought us a bucket with prosecco in it and we toasted our engagement. We both had joy beaming out from us. We spent the last hour of 2021 celebrating our engagement, before the hope that came with the stroke of midnight and the New Year arrived. We had a wedding to plan and arrangements to make.

I was in charge of organising the wedding because Clare was busy working and didn't have the time that I had. One of my first priorities though was to draw my dad. I got the main things in place for the wedding, but mostly spent my time perfecting my drawing of him. I was in a place in my head to do it now and felt like it was the right time. I now had the love in me when I thought of him to have the patience and perseverance to do it. The drawings I did of my parents are two of my life's greatest achievements.

At the wedding itself, which was only about four months later, I stood waiting in the church in disbelief that I was getting married. Clare had bought me a pin with my parents' photos on it and a little guardian angel in between them, which sat on the outside of my jacket breast. I constantly looked at it and checked that it still looked right. That it was neat, and they were visible, all three of them.

The church was full that afternoon, and the anticipation was building as I waited at the front with my best man, Nick. Finally, she arrived. After a long pause, the first notes of Hoppipola played through the speakers, which is a really emotional and uplifting piece of music. I knew they wouldn't start walking in until the second wave as I had instructed them, to build the anticipation in the church. My brother was in the foyer with them monitoring the music and keeping them calm and patient.

"Not yet. You look gorgeous. Nearly there. He's waiting for you. Just breathe," he said to Clare.

Then the second wave of the music started.

"Ok, that's your cue."

My brother confirmed to the bride's maids and Clare, along with a thumbs up and a nod. I looked over my right shoulder and saw the bride's maids walking in, so I looked forward again. It was happening!

The music was emotional, the energy in the church was emotional, and I couldn't believe that something so good, so wonderful, so utterly amazing was happening to me. I had come to believe that nothing good would happen to me or for me. I was gutted that my parents weren't there to see it and share it with me. I adjusted them again on my chest. Then Clare arrived next to me on my left, and I looked at her with a big smile on my face and moist eyes as I reached out my hand to hers. She looked gorgeous.

"You didn't think she was going to come in did you?" Steve, the pastor, said to the congregation. They laughed in response and relaxed in their seats. We moved onto the first song, *'O'Come to the Altar'*, which we chose to set the tone for the wedding, both in terms of being uplifting and the message behind it. As it also turned out, Steve's sermon was based on 1 Corinthians thirteen, and the greatness of love, and shared love in marriage. It had a beautiful sentiment and added to the occasion because of its content, and because of my relationship with that chapter of the Bible.

When it came to the vows Clare and I had Bible verses selected to read to each other. The extreme joy and sadness that I felt was too much for me to handle though. I struggled to see the words and talk properly as I read my chosen Bible verses to Clare. I kept apologising to her that I was so emotional, and for having to stop then go again.

"Get a grip Mart." She quipped leaning around the mic.

"I know, sorry, I can't help it." All I could think about was my mum and Dad not being there to see it.

The obvious choice for me to go with would have been 1 Corinthians, chapter thirteen, but I chose to look at verses which were less obvious and still had meaning for me and Clare. After hearing Steve's sermon, I was glad I did. So, instead I read to her;

"Haven't you read," he replied, 'that at the beginning the Creator 'made them male and female,' and said, 'For this reason a man will leave his father and mother and be united to his wife, and the two will become one flesh'? So they are no longer two, but one flesh. Therefore, what God has joined together - let no one separate", (Matthew 19: 4-6).

I thought of my parents as I read it out through my tears and straining throat. I continued to my second verse.

"Let the morning bring me word of your unfailing love, for I have put my trust in you. Show me the way I should go, for to you I entrust my life" (Psalm 143: 8).

Then it was Clare's turn to read to me, who was much more composed and able than I had been.

"Where you go I will go, and where you stay I will stay. Your people will be my people and your God my God. Where you die I will die, and there will I be buried. May the Lord deal with me, be it ever so severely, if even death separates you and me", (Ruth 1: 16-17).

What a choice she had made, what a commitment for her to make to me. I felt humbled hearing her read it to me in front of our people.

After the vows we went over to a table, which was in front of the kitchen hatch that served the toast on a Saturday morning after Parkrun, to sign the legal documents. As we did that, we had '*Songbirds*' by Eva Cassidy playing on the big screen. Clare's son broke down sobbing, joined by his younger sister. The words of the song were perfect for the moment and embodied the emotion and sentiment as we signed for our union.

The plan next, was to get the congregation clapping in unison before we left the church. The video on the screen was changed to the song that would play us out, '*Nobody*' by Casting Crowns. CLAP, STOMP, CLAP, CLAP, STOMP played out from the speakers as the song began. Clare and I, now stood at the front, clapped in time with such conviction that everybody else felt compelled to join us I'm sure. The hall was filled by the sound of the song and everybody in it clapping in time. When the song had finished singing the chorus again, Clare turned to me with a big smile on her face;

"Shall we."

I nodded. She put her hand in mine and we slowly walked out of the church with the song still playing and accompanied by the percussion of the congregations' hands loudly clapping together as one. It was amazing!

We walked down the aisle, through the heart of our family and friends, either side of us were big smiles with little nods and winks. We then turned left towards the doors through which I had first walked five years earlier, and Clare had made her entrance as my bride. My aunty, my dad's sister, was stood on our right at the back of the church as we slowly made our way past her. She briefly paused from clapping as my eyes met with hers and held her fists up in front of her in celebration. With joy splashed across her face she looked at me and said happily.

"You did it!"

That was all that needed to be said. The smile on my face exploded into laughter as we walked out to the music and joy, which cloaked us as we arrived into the warm sunshine as a married couple. Our celebration continued back at the golf club where I was a member. Clare and I were driven there by Nick who, after hearing me comment on Steve's sermon, reminded me that his birthday was on the thirteenth. I chuckled and looked at Clare because she knew how difficult it had been for me to choose a best man. As I stood in front of the room to give my speech, my drawings of my mum and dad sat behind and on either side of me. It just felt right to have them there. I proudly introduced our wedding party to Mrs Clare Ridley and the whole room toasted her. We performed our first dance which we had practiced for weeks; the dance floor was later packed as we danced the night away to the live band, who were brilliant. It was truly the best day of my life!

Chapter 13

Lessons Learned

The loss of our baby was an ever-present shadow in our new marriage. We were trying to get pregnant again, but it was an endeavour and topic which caused a lot of stress and strain in our home and in our relationship. Our mindsets were not aligned in our approach to it. I was more laid back about it and went more with a 'let's see what happens' approach. I was leaving it to God and if it was meant to happen then it would happen, if not then we could still live a good life as a married couple. Clare on the other hand was taking every supplement she could and monitoring herself constantly in order to make herself as much of an optimum home for a new pregnancy as possible. She was focussed on every detail of fertility and getting pregnant.

She read that women who suffer a miscarriage often get pregnant again soon afterwards, usually within the first six months. So as those first six months went by she was more and more distressed and upset when the end of her cycle arrived again. It was like she was reliving the loss in some form every month, and grieving the lack of success in getting pregnant over and over. Grieving the distance that remained between her reality and the picture she had clear in her mind of us with our child. Getting pregnant hadn't been on our radar until we did. By the time we had lost it again Clare had seen the movie of it in her mind, she had pictured our life raising our child and she'd felt motherhood in her body. She was now desperate to get it back. Our marriage began with us on an emotional rollercoaster which derailed once a month.

This two-sided coin with the miscarriage on one side and infertility on the other seemed to be put in the juke box of our marriage on a daily, or at least weekly basis. It put a lot of strain on us as a couple and as individuals from the start. Clare was taking it very hard that we couldn't get pregnant again despite all of the effort she was going to. While I stressed about how we would cope financially if we did get pregnant. The tension, stress and emotional ups and downs of it was hard. I hadn't allowed myself to watch the movie of me being a parent in my mind like Clare had, I'd cut it off at the pregnancy ending in the early stages. My mind was more matter of fact about it than Clare's. The biological process had failed in my mind whereas our future was being kept from us in Clare's mind.

Prior to meeting Clare I had mentally written myself off as a parent, so for me I think it was back to life as normal. Of course the pregnancy didn't work out. I'm not meant to be a dad. That's for my cousins and my friends, not me. I would have loved to be a dad though. I'm sure I would have cried as I held my baby for the first time, just like my dad did when he held me apparently. I can only imagine the joy and emotions that go through a parent's body as they hold their tiny creation for the first time. I would have loved to raise a person, taught them things, encouraged them and supported them as they found their way. I would have loved to play with them and laugh with them, to be known as Daddy or Dad. I would have loved it all. I would have been a good dad too.

It soon became time for Christmas again, one year after losing our child. How could Christmas' ever be a time of celebration for us again after that? After losing a child on Boxing Day. A time to be merry and in good cheer, not with that in my mind I don't think. Of course, as Christians, it's a time for us to celebrate the birth of Jesus, but even that was difficult to do. Christmas will be tainted for us for the rest of our lives, how could it not be? For the first one after the miscarriage, I suggested that we go away somewhere, and thankfully Clare's mother, Caroline, was up for us staying with her for Christmas. So we were able to spend Christmas away from home and in an environment devoid of emotional triggers of what had happened the year before. We would just need to cope with the memories in our minds from twelve months earlier. We managed ok for the most part. It was good that Clare was kept busy helping her mum.

Over the course of the year it had become apparent to me that getting married was the easy part, being married was the hard part, very hard. I wish I could tell you that everything has worked out lovely and that all my dreams have come true, but then that's not how it works and not the point of this book. I'm not writing it to tell you a story of despair to greatness. It's not about look at me then and then look at me now. After leaving the police I became a golf coach, which was something I'd always wanted to do but had been put off by other people. I've enjoyed it too but it hasn't resolved my difficulties with work.

I now know myself and who I am better than ever before, and as I sit here writing I await my official NHS assessment for autism in a matter of weeks. It's taken about eighteen months to get here from being notified of my assessment. I really hope that they will diagnose me but I know that they might not because there is so much emphasis placed on childhood, and I haven't got anyone who can really testify to what I was like as a child. So I'm taking Clare with me to testify about what I'm like and who I am now as an adult. Either way we are both sure that I am autistic and that won't change from what they conclude. I know, we know. I'm just hoping to get a piece of paper which makes it official and might open doors for me to get support or something. Or show that it's not just my opinion at least.

When I went down on my knees and prayed to a God that I didn't believe in I had no idea that I was probably autistic. I didn't know who I was. I knew who I thought I was, I knew how I thought the world saw me. I was nothing short of a disappointment and a let-down, a recurring story of failure and grief. A person that was just waiting for the next terrible thing to come crashing round the corner and knock me off my feet again. I was hopeless and worthless. I just wanted to tag out, jump off, exit, escape. I didn't want to do this anymore, I'd had enough.

Since getting back up from my knees after that prayer God showed me, through Jude, the joys that can be available in life from the smallest of things such as what you are having for dinner or kicking a sponge ball around in a church hall. That whether everything is for you or against you is dependent upon how you see things not the circumstances you are in themselves. God showed me, through Parkrun, how exercise can help and how a community can encourage each other even as they overtake each other. That people can run the same race and yet still be on the same side, clapping each other on and congratulating people for just turning up, for just being there. That having them with us is enough.

God showed me that prayer brings peace and a connection with him. Through certain numbers he showed me that he was with me, that he's always been with me and waiting for me to speak to him. Through church and the Bible he has taught me a better way to live, through his corrections in my life and answers to prayer he has taught me who I am and who I should strive to be. He has shown me who he is and what he wants to do for me, that all of his intentions for me and my life are good. That he wants the best for me.

God has shown me that love is the most important thing in life, even more important than faith or hope because without love they are fruitless. He has shown me how much he loves me and wants me to love others. He brought one of the best forms of love to me in Clare, who is one of the most loving people I have ever known. He has shown me that money is a dangerous thing which can corrupt us and muddy the love that can be available to us. The chase for money or protection of money typically just denies people opportunities to receive or give love in its purist form.

It's the chase for money and status, the chase for the approval of others and the comparisons between myself and others, between my current self and past opportunities which has caused much of my inner turmoil about who I am. I'm now a grown man, but I'm still protecting the boy I was, still trying to make up for his mistakes and failures. Still striving to attain the things that he felt were needed for Dad to be proud of him and for him to feel respected by other people.

God has shown me that my lifelong search to belong was ignorant of the fact that I already belonged to him. That he created me the way I am and that I am living out his plan for me so that I can mature and grow as a person - destined for the heavenly bliss of eternity with him and in a world where love is abundant rather than scarce. Where everyone is on the same side and everyone belongs.

Ultimately God has shown and proven his truth to me and that he is with me to help and support me through whatever happens in my life on Earth. I now know the peace of looking to him and of following his guidance and direction in everything that I do. He has shown me the peace available from giving up the control of my life and trusting in his higher purpose for my time in this world. God has shown me that he is my safe place and that he is my ultimate trampoline, where no matter how far I fall he will help me to bounce back up again, and again. He will comfort me and then pull me up from despair and suffering, giving me the hope and strength to rise to my feet and walk forward in faith once more. In fact he will show me how my suffering brings faith, hope and love to me and others.

Earlier this year, 2023, I finally arranged to scatter my gran's ashes. Uncertainty of what to do with them when she died, life and struggles had got in the way, but it was well overdue. Me and my brother went back to the venue where we had stood alone for her funeral service in 2020. They had an area called Daffodil Hill where they scattered ashes, and we could have a small service as it was done. The daffodils weren't out yet, but it was still a nice setting with several tall trees dotted about and a stream at the bottom of the hill which ran across relative to the face of the hill.

As we made our way down the hill, I was struck by all the patches of grey on the ground. Patches of grey dust that used to be people and now there they were on the earth while we walked through and around them. We went down to the bottom where there was more grass and less areas of grey, and we were closer to the stream. It was a really nice setting with ribbons of sun light falling to the ground around us through the gaps in the branches of the trees. The water in the stream sparkled as it trickled past.

The Officiant then delivered a small service which lasted no more than one minute, before he scattered our gran onto the grass. There she was now too, a patch of grey dust that used to be the person we stayed with as kids and saw at Christmas. The person that brought my mum into the world. Now just dust on the ground. I looked at her and felt exposed and vulnerable to my own mortality and the inevitable ending of my own journey to Daffodil Hill or into a hole in the ground.

It caused me to think of the Bible where it said that God made us from the dust of the ground and that we will return to dust one day. As I looked around me and down at where my gran was now scattered on the ground the reality of that really hit me. 'That will be me one day, I need to make sure that I live in the best way before I get there', I thought. I now know that to do that I must follow Jesus and worship God, that I must pray and live by the spirit within me.

The story told in this book was written by God, I just tried to tell it as well as I could. I can't believe I'm actually going to publish the book I knew I had in me and have been trying to write for many years. It's finally happened though because this was the right time, this was the right book; and writing and publishing it was irresistible to me. Ultimately the answers that I was searching for were in chapter 13, the chapter you've just read. Which was added at the editors' request, it was not a conscious act of mine, I didn't even realise there was thirteen chapters until the editors told me.

A couple of weeks ago I was at Parkrun with Matt, you know, the mate that originally invited me to go for that first run in 2017. It occurred to me that morning how significant one of his tattoos was to this story, because I remembered that he had a tattoo of the number thirteen. I asked him about it, and he showed it to me on the inside of his upper arm. When I asked why he had it, he said that he believed it brought good fortune. It certainly did for me!

You might also be interested to know that I have now been diagnosed as autistic. I am officially autistic. So, I am now clearer on who I am and how to live than I've been in forty three years of my life so far. However long I have left, I will endeavour to apply what I have learnt while I can, and *Before the Dust Settles*.

Praise and thanks to God.

"In Jesus' name, amen."

Now and again I have been inspired to write poems for church. This one was inspired to be read out during the Easter service.

<u>The Lights of the Runway</u>

From heaven down to earth,
From his throne to a human birth,
From glory to being surrounded by sin,
From God's side to knowing what was to become of him.

God's son transformed into a human child,
Born for the people that fled from the Nile,
Brought up by parents who were lower than he,
As he was raised on a cross for all to see.

Following his Father's plan, sweating blood,
The human God pleaded to be relieved of his duty if he could,
But the Father's will remained his will,
Which was reaffirmed to him in their moments of quiet and still.

Betrayed as he knew by his disciples,
Just to teach us more lessons from his Bible,
Let down so often by those that he chose,
Undervalued so often, by those that he knows.

Pure white polluted by black hearts,
Forced to enter hell after his spirit would depart,
Innocent but for the guilty filth that saturated his soul,
Beaten faceless by the world he saved, as recorded on his scroll.

The Son following the Father as an example to you,
The Son sacrificed by the Father instead of you,
The Son raised from the death of his body and your sin,
Jesus Christ, don't we owe so much to him!

Acknowledgements

I would like to acknowledge my biggest fan, my mum, and my hero, my dad, and thank them for everything that they did for me.

Thank you to my wife, Clare, for her support, encouragement and extensive help with writing this book.

Thank you to my brother for being my brother and his help with the book too.

I also want to thank my publisher Cassandra Welford for her guidance and for proposing the title of the book.

Thank you to Alison for her skilled help with editing the book.

Thank you to John and Naomi for allowing me to share their family with you.

A big thank you to Matt for inviting me to that first run and picking me up each week.

After that it's impossible to include everyone. So, thank you to the pastors and members of Park Church, Hope church, my family, friends and everyone that knows me.

About the Author

Martin Ridley, who lives in Newcastle-Under-Lyme, has been described as inspiring. Despite the trauma, loss and grief that he has been through, and the challenges he has faced all through his life. He keeps going and falling forwards while looking to help other people where he can. He has been hoping to write a book that will help people for several years, and now he has finally done it. As it turned out the story he was to write was his own. Martin's mission is to encourage people to explore Christianity; to help people that have or are suffering like he has; to champion Autistic people, and encourage people generally to talk and share their struggles more.

Contact Martin at

martinridley.author@gmail.com

www.ingramcontent.com/pod-product-compliance
Lightning Source LLC
Chambersburg PA
CBHW071349080526
44587CB00017B/3027